gambit
INTERNATIONAL THEATRE REVIEW

Volume 10   Number 37

D1344002

Executive Editor & Founder CAV. ROBERT RIETTY
Editor JOHN CALDER
Assistant Editor DAVID ROPER
Production & Design CHRISTOPHER CRESEY

SUBSCRIPTION RATES: Sterling 4 issues £7.50
USA and Canada: $16.50

Manuscripts to be considered for publication may be submitted, but these can only be returned if a stamped addressed envelope or sufficient postage in International Reply Coupons is enclosed.

Letters from readers on any material appearing in GAMBIT will be welcomed and should be addressed to the Magazine Editor. Readers are also invited to submit articles to be considered for publication.

Correspondence should be addressed to:
GAMBIT, 18 Brewer Street, London W1R 4AS

ISBN 0 7145 3830 2

The Publishers gratefully acknowledge financial assistance from the Arts Council of Great Britain.

Typeset by Gilbert Composing Services, Leighton Buzzard, in 9 point Press Roman
Printed by The Hillman Press, Frome, Somerset.

EDITORIAL: THE BEGINNING OF THE CRUNCH

Although the Arts Council received a 12% increase for the financial year 1981-82, they have cut 41 of their 'clients' from the list of bodies to which they give subsidy. The great majority of these are theatrical organizations or publications. Some of these bodies have been brave attempts to bring some form of theatrical or musical activity to an area that was previously a cultural desert. The Arts Council must know that it takes several years to establish a new festival, theatre or arts centre, and the pattern seldom varies much: when the new enterprise starts there is both local and national publicity because a new venture is interesting and newsworthy, and the enthusiasm of the organisers becomes infectious; then, usually during the second year, there is a dropping off because the curiosity has worn off, the local philistines have started to attack and those whose interest was minor anyway have fallen off. Then comes the gradual building of real support, partly in answer to the crisis and partly because the educational and awareness-creating function of any cultural activity has begun to get through to a number of local people as they realize that their lives have been genuinely enhanced.

To withdraw support from such organizations as the two-year old Buxton Festival, the Crewe Theatre Trust and the Little Missenden Festival is to ensure that there will be little to stimulate the lively minds of the area and that the inevitable drift to the metropolis will continue. The new policy is obviously anti-regional and barely conceals a bureaucratic dislike for organizations that live on enthusiasm and are too young to have yet developed knowhow of how bureaucracy functions with the jargon that accompanies it. Those who are well paid to hand out subsidy are not necessarily interested in the arts themselves and often tend to dislike enthusiasts whose interest is so great that they will work—and work hard—for love.

But even more disturbing is the list of theatre companies and theatre magazines, established for years, with a good track record for producing a quality product and for stimulating audiences and readers, who are now left high and dry. What this second category of 'clients' has in common is that they have a radical anti-authoritarian bias that inevitably was going to make them a target for a government such as the present one. Inter-Action Trust is a good example. Created by Ed Berman in the sixties, it has become much more than an organization presenting plays with an anti-Conservative political bias. It runs an arts centre for children, it tours productions for every age group, it is involved in play groups and in the political rallying of protesters against local authority blight or other burning issues. It was a great asset to the people of Camden Town, especially with young children, and the Almost Free Theatre in Rupert Street performed some astonishing plays. In addition, Ed Berman succedded in breaking down the barriers between British and American Equity so that his two touring companies—containing an equal number of British and American actors, without stars—could perform in both countries. And it was obvious that Berman and his helpers got very little out of it themselves except the satisfaction of doing a variety of good jobs well.

Now it is not just the smaller theatrical groups who put on plays with a political bias or theme, or works that are daring in their presentation of sex, violence or taboo subjects of the day. Sir Peter Hall at the National has stuck his neck out as far as anyone and been much criticized for it, but the National Theatre is now our top theatrical institution, well staffed with bureaucrats and fluent in the jargon. But that does not mean that the National would be immune from attack for long, although in their case the attack would consist not of withdrawal of financial support, but of the dismissal of those personalities who commission and produce controversial plays and are too open in voicing their opposition to the direction that society is taking. The National, the Royal Shakespeare and the Royal Court have nurtured and built up an extraordinary generation of political playwrights who have done much to create awareness of the dangers that British society is facing. In 1977, in GAMBIT 31, we prophesied what is happening now, saying that 'by 1980 we shall probably be looking back with enviousness and nostaligia' and hoped that 'the subsidy-giving bodies will resist the temptation to censor.' Well, the crunch has now begun and it will not be long before heads roll in our large theatrical institutions, to be replaced by safe men willing to put on safe plays. For two decades London has had the most exciting drama in the world, only occasionally rivalled by the French or German, while New York remains the home of slick musicals, mindless and anodine situational comedies and only very rarely is there a short run of a play of intellectual merit or current relevance. But the retreat has started, and GAMBIT with its independent point of view and dislike of bureaucracy and censorship is itself one of the victims.

It is also interesting to see which institutions, large or small, are getting 'significantly increased levels of subsidy'. We cannot criticize the list, but there are many institutions that have never aspired to the levels of interest and quality of some of the companies now sacrificed, and few of them have ever been controversial. It is again worth noting that every theatrical magazine with a serious point of view has lost Arts Council support, so that it will be increasingly difficult for British playwrights who find that their new plays are not performed to find a platform or advocates for their work. And now the dismissal of Norman St John Stevas, probably the most civilized member of the Thatcher cabinet, virtually ensures that the arts will be downgraded in national importance. The challenge is now to find a way, as the arts always have in history, to outwit censors and subsidisers, and find a way of getting their message through to the intelligent public. It is even possible that some artists who have had too easy a time will benefit from less food and more fire in their bellies.

John Calder

TRAD TOM POPS IN

Tom Stoppard in interview with David Gollob and David Roper

Thirteen years on and *Rosencrantz and Guildenstern* are still very much alive. *The Real Inspector Hound* is still nosing around, though *Dirty Linen* has finally come off, after an almost interminable hanging at the Arts Theatre in London. All round the world, in France, in Canada, in the States, the plays that first established Stoppard's reputation as a comic playwright with a message continue to delight, tease, and draw audiences.

But lately Tom's work seems to have modulated away from the glitter of Wildean disengagement, biting into the more meaty domains of freedom of expression in Czechoslovakia and freedom of the press in the embattled U.K. More matter with less art? Or a desire for art that matters more?

However you look at it, there is a distinctly politically conscious cloud darkening the later plays, and when Tom kindly consented to be interviewed by GAMBIT, I thought this would be an interesting area to probe around in, especially as the late Kenneth Tynan's article on Stoppard (reprinted on page19) was lying in front of me, inviting questions about what Tynan had called Stoppard's shift from withdrawal to engagement.

GOLLOB: Let's plunge in . . . with a bathing anecdote. This is an
apocryphal anecdote about A.J. Ayer going swimming with some other philosophy dons at a men only bathing area on the Cherwell. They are frolicking around starkers when all of a sudden these girls go by in a punt. All reach for their towels in a mad rush to cover their private parts except for Ayer who covers his head. Do you know the story?
STOPPARD: Yes, and the story is a lot older than Freddy Ayer.
GOLLOB: Is it?
STOPPARD: Yes, I mean I suppose it may have happened to somebody sometime but I'm not even sure that it did. It's a story told about Oxford dons, sometimes about a particular one and it's usually set in a sort of Edwardian England when I suppose naked men were even more shocking, but let's assume it happened to Freddy as well and— I'll take the supplementary if you like.
GOLLOB: I grabbed this little anecdote because I'd like to explore the role of the disinterested play of the intellect in your work and ask

you if we should see the thematic darkening and return to naturalism characterized by your most recent work—*Night and Day,* for example— as a kind of movement from withdrawal to involvement, as some have put it . . . as if you were covering your cleverness in order to force it to serve a more serious moral purpose. In other words, is this your response to the kind of criticism that has been levelled against you by people like Tynan and Walter Kerr: that *Travesties* is, for example a 'three decker bus going nowhere' or Kerr's description—'an intellectual hummingbird unable to light anywhere' . . . Were you consciously reacting to this kind of criticism of insubstantiality?

STOPPARD: Not consciously, as I was about to say. If it is a response, it's a deeply subconscious one. All that I'm aware of is that I had practical reasons for writing *Professional Foul* which is the first more or less realistic play I've written for ages, and is so, as far as I was concerned at the time of writing, because I knew I was writing for television. The attraction of unexpected, unnatural, or 'unnaturalistic' things happening on a stage is precisely that they **are** happening on a **stage.** The surprising effects depend partly on the audience's barely conscious knowledge of the limitations of a stage. A lot of things I like very much as pieces of staging in *Jumpers* or *Travesties* would be more or less pointless if you were making a movie of either of those plays. When I came to writing a play for TV I felt something of the same thing. I should make it clear that I'm speaking with hindsight knowledge now—in sitting down to write a play one doesn't really examine all these options—but I do know that I just thought, without even having to bother to think about it, that *Professional Foul* ought to be naturalistic, and that TV is best for that sort of play, and that it's impact should be to do with human relationships and the way things are said and to whom they're said and not to do with the sort of ambushes I like to or did like to set up on a stage.

And then, *Night and Day,* the last stage-play I've written, is also a naturalistic play. I had a perfectly sound explanation for that as well, and a very mundane one. It was a play which I wrote for Michael Codron because I'd promised him a play ten years previously, and there were a number of considerations which were more or less self-conscious ones, to do with one set, and not too many actors, so that Michael Codron would be able to do it as a West End manager. I mean, giving him a play which started with fourteen acrobats wouldn't have pleased him. And because it was a play about journalism, one of the few times I've ever drawn on my own experience, even secondhand experience, because I didn't work on Fleet Street, I wanted to do a naturalistic play.

I was also interested by the way journalists tend to ape their fictitious models. It's a certain way of behaving which derives from 'tough' films. Of course, in naturalism there is a reciprocal thing between the model and life, and in thinking yes, yes, a play about journalists of some sort, again without a great deal of thought, I fell into a way of thinking about the material which led to a naturalistic play. Sorry to be so garrulous, but your question contains a lot of elements and I don't want to short-change you . . . . .

6

GOLLOB: Can I just try and focus it a bit? I located something that intrigued me in your critical preface to *Every Good Boy Deserves Favour* and *Professional Foul* where you describe an incident when Vladimir Bukovsky having been released from the Soviet Union attended a rehearsal of this play about him. There was a certain moment of malaise or embarassment when the real thing, the real life issue came into contact with this very wonderful entertainment. I was wondering if this was a kind of fulcrum for you, seeing that you have mentioned *Professional Foul* as a naturalistic play, whereas *Every Good Boy* in its very playful way also dealt with a serious issue.

STOPPARD: The embarrassment which you refer to when Bukovsky attended a rehearsal wasn't really to do with the playfulness or otherwise of *Every Good Boy*. As a matter of fact, when he came we weren't doing one of the playful parts. Ian McKellen, one of the actors involved, playing one of the more serious characters, was in fact doing the least playful speech in the piece. So the feeling of unease which I got—which Ian got: as far as I can remember he couldn't carry on—wasn't to do with the discrepancy between the mood of the art and the mood of the real situation which this man represented. No, it was to do with the discrepancy between art and life full stop. And I think one would have felt the same thing if *King Lear* had been based on fact and Gloucester had wandered in—the same sort of embarrassment would have ensued. You know, what we were engaged in was a sort of artifice, and one knows that it's an artifice, I mean the whole **point** of it is that it is an artifice, not the point of the piece but the point of us being there together, was to simulate something, not to live it. And it was that discordance which suddenly went 'clang!'

Every Good Boy is about a serious subject. It's not a naturalistic piece, it's an odd sort of a piece that was defined by the situation it was to be performed in and by the people it was to be performed by, namely the orchestra. I can sum up this whole area of question, without necessarily suggesting it should be fore-closed, by saying it is not the case that one examines the nature of a subject matter and thereupon decides on using a certain kind of form . . . Let me just think a minute . . . Let me just start that again. The equation which I would disavow is that any serious, involved, engaged playwriting is equated by this author with naturalism—no. The plays which I've written more recently which tend to be naturalistic and also tend to engage themselves with serious immediate matters are not exhibiting a relationship between those two facts . . . as far as I am honestly aware . . . if I can just add a rider to explain more fully what I mean.

See, at bottom, *Professional Foul* and *Jumpers* can each be described as a play about a moral philosopher preoccupied with the true nature of absolute morality, trying to separate absolute values from local ones and local situations. That description would apply to either play, yet one is a rampant farce and the other is a piece of naturalistic TV drama.

GOLLOB: *Professional Foul* also seems to bear certain similarities with the existentialist drama, the Sartrian theatre of situations, in the way that the central character becomes more aware of his global situation in terms of other men at grips with, engaged in the problems of life. He is prodded by a brutal awakening of consciousness—he goes to visit his former philosophy student in his flat in Prague and gets cornered by the police, missing this frivolous football match which is the real reason for his visit—he is prodded by this brutal awakening, his new consciousness, to engage himself in a moral action: he changes the speech he was going to deliver.

STOPPARD: Yes.

GOLLOB: And if you'll allow me to expand on this, I feel there is something emblematic about this speech he has changed, from what to what, which suggests a kind of change in your writing, in that, taking another character like McKendrick with his brilliant 'Catastrophe Theory' and its mathematical, verbal beauty, this disinterested player of the mind who fundamentally is an ass and a boor is contrasted with someone like Anderson who becomes engaged in a quest for some kind of fundamental ethical basis based on something that has touched him personally . . . and I think there is a movement away from this, well some people have said trivial side of your writing . . . do you see what I mean?

STOPPARD: I do. However, taking your idea about Anderson's lecture and the change it goes through and about there being something emblematic in this, that's not really so clear because we don't know what his speech would have been. What we do know is derived from his conversation in the hotel corridor with the Czech boy—in other words Anderson produces his arguments about why he shouldn't act, why he shouldn't interfere in Czech politics, and then what happens is something extremely simple . . . he just brushes up against the specific reality of the mother and the child, especially the child.

You can make a case for what you're saying, but wielding Occam's razor upon it, the same thing can be said in a much simpler way. What happens is that he's got a perfectly respectable philosophical thesis and he encounters a mother and a child who are victims of this society, and it cuts through all the theory. It's as though there are two moralties: one to do with systems of government and an alternative morality to do with relationships between individuals. The latter is govenred by instinctive feelings about what good and bad behaviour consist of and an instant and instinctive recognition of each when they occur. The pay-off really is that when Anderson puts his friend at risk by hiding the essay which he is smuggling in his colleague's briefcase, he says something like, 'I thought you would approve'! This is the man's public stance. And of course his colleague makes the same discovery that it's all very well in the bloody textbooks, but this is me, I could be in that jail, this is my briefcase, you bastard!

So it's more to do with a man being educated by experience beyond the education he's received from thinking.

GOLLOB: Good, but if you'll allow me to pursue this, because I like digging, the text of the speech Anderson substitutes bears an uncanny resemblance to an argument—if I'm not mistaken—in a Havel play . . .

STOPPARD: Really!

GOLLOB: I think it might be from 'Conspirators' . . . (Ed. note: In fact Gollob was referring to a letter by Havel, quoted in Tynan's article, about *Conspirators*.)

STOPPARD: Have you ever read *Conspirators?*

GOLLOB: No, I haven't.

STOPPARD: Oh, because I've never seen *Conspirators*.

GOLLOB: Maybe this is a rather curious coincidence, then?

STOPPARD: Not that curious, is it? I mean it's not that curious that somebody like Havel would have a similar argument.

GOLLOB: 'Truth is guaranteed only by the full weight of humanity behind it.' Am I quoting from you, or am I quoting from Havel?

STOPPARD: It must be Havel.

GOLLOB: Looking at *Professional Foul* from the outside, it sounds almost as if when Anderson begins speaking with a different voice, it's also Stoppard who is beginning to inflect his voice differently, taking an ethical stance with more force. I felt a remarkable sort of kinship was being illustrated here.

STOPPARD: In fact I've had a feeling of kinship with Havel for a hell of a long time. When I read *The Garden Party* about twelve years ago, I just thought he was somebody who wrote like I would like to write if I was writing on the same subject. There are playwrights one admires because one could never do what they do, and there are those one admires because one **could** do exactly what they do and would wish to. But as far as Anderson's statement being the shadow on the wall of something that has happened to me—straining the natural courtesy which makes the interviewee wish the interviewer to have got it right, I don't think you have.

The reason why Anderson talks the way he does is because people like him to talk like that. I can honestly say that I have held Anderson's final view on the subject for years and years, and years before Anderson ever existed. I think something has made you believe that the arc of my development has intersected with the arc of the fictitious character's development and they cross when he speaks.

GOLLOB: I don't. I'm just constructing a pattern. It's what critics do.

STOPPARD: I wanted to write about somebody coming from England to a totalitarian society, brushing up against it, and getting a little soiled and a little wiser. I spent a long time wondering what to do . . . and I thought: a ballroom dancing team, with those wonderful ladies in tangerine tulle . . . 'Come Dancing' in Prague . . . but I was really interested in the moral implications, and the equation just simplified itself until the formation dancers became moral philosophers. What you've got then is a desire to write about a moral philosopher who goes to Prague. An appeal is made to him by a former student, the appeal is rejected, he gets his nose rubbed in it slightly, learns, and acts. But what he learns isn't something which the writer is simultaneously learning in the course of writing the play. On the contrary, that's the end objective of the original desire to write the play.

GOLLOB: I think you once said—and this is supposed to be a quote—
'. . . . the ideas are the product . . .'

STOPPARD: (coming to the rescue) Yes I know what you mean, and it has the overstatement of most epigrams: 'the ideas are the end-product of the play, not the other way round'. That used to be something I said with complete sincerity because after I had written *Rosencrantz and Guildenstern* I encountered over the next few years all kinds of interpretations of the events of the play, and it seemed to me that the play had somehow created all these ideas in the mind of the watcher and so were in that sense the end-product of a play about two Elizabethan courtiers trapped by the action of *Hamlet*. I was at some pains to try and say that I didn't start off with certain abstract ideas and then look around for a vessel to contain them. And I did tend to plug that because I found—and still find—many people (I'm thinking of students and school children) who write to one with the firm conviction that there's some sort of secret code which I know and they don't and which they're supposed to work out. But of course what you were quoting stopped being applicable round about the time I started writing *Jumpers*.

There the play was the end-product of an idea as much as the converse. I wanted to write about the dispute between somebody who thinks that morality is an absolute and somebody who thinks that it's a convention which we have evolved like the rules of tennis, and which can be altered.

ROPER: Are you familiar with a recent TV play about a writer who was interested in a dissident?

STOPPARD: No, unfortunately I didn't know anything about it until I read the review of it.

ROPER: It bore curious resemblances to what you yourself have done but it made precisely the opposite point from the one you've just corrected. First one took one's dissident and then made something of it.

STOPPARD: I haven't entirely corrected it, because *Every Good Boy* is a play which does something like that. There is another sort of writing where you could write a play set in Arundel Gardens which says something about dissidents but only had us in it and never mentioned the word 'dissidents'. It could be about this piece of cake.

I think the thing which I haven't quite said is that the proposition which you began with and which has led to this entire forty minutes is fundamentally true. It's actually true that I began writing at a time when the climate was such that theatre seemed to exist for the specific purpose of commenting on our own society directly. Temperamentally this didn't suit me, because I would much rather have written *The Importance of Being Earnest* than . . . than . . .

GOLLOB: *(breaking in)* Than *Look Back in Anger*?

STOPPARD: Yes. Well, hang on, that's more complicated because *Look Back in Anger* is full of wonderful speeches which I would like to have been able to write. And I don't think it would be nice to name the sort of play which is engaged with society but which doesn't contain anything I admire, and there are such plays. And so, I took on a sort of 'travelling pose' which exaggerated my insecurity about not being able to fit into this scheme, and I tended to overcorrect, as though in some peculiar way *Earnest* was actually more important than a play which grappled, right? So, what you say is fundamentally true . . . I did, I had to change as time went by, and began looking for a marriage between the play of ideas and the work of wit.

ROPER: But there's a further paradox: if you start writing about society then you once again assume one of these absolute models. If you then move to writing a play about an individual are you then, in shifting away from absolute positions, writing about Man, about Society. Are you then denying yourself the possibility of appealing to a majority audience?

STOPPARD: Well, it's generally true, isn't it, that one's appeal to an audience is less to do with what one is saying than how one is saying it, and in that respect there is surprisingly little choice to be made by a writer. Whatever comes to your mill, you grind it the same. There's only one way you **can** write in the end, and that's the way you **do** write . . . the difference between *Night and Day* and *Travesties* is more to do with structure than how I write.

I find that people who saw these two plays are divided along those who congratulate me on getting past the 'hummingbird' phase and those who say 'What are you doing? It's all naturalistic, with a beginning, a middle, and an end!' But there's no external position where you say, 'I think that in view of what so-and-so's been writing about me I'd better get to grips with something recognisable and do it properly.' Nothing like that happens . . . and though I haven't begun a new play and have only the vaguest idea of the area I'd like to write about, it's perfectly possible that it will be a play that will disappoint people who liked *Night and Day* or *Professional Foul.*

GOLLOB: To change the subject slightly, Tom Lehrer was in town recently for the opening of a new show, *Tomfoolery* and I overheard him say that there is no question of him going back to writing songs—that he feels this sort of humour is no longer possible. That the flippancy of tone informing these satires of literally burning human issues is *mal à propos*, as if the bottom had fallen out of the humour market.

STOPPARD: They're nostalgia.

GOLLOB: Right, and they refer us back to the period in which they were conceived, just as *Rosencrantz and Guildenstern* is doing now in London and Paris.

STOPPARD: Actually I want to go to Paris, because it sounds fascinating. They've got three actors and a lot of puppets. God knows what they're doing, I'd love to see it.

11

GOLLOB: I think there's been a general darkening since then, and I'm not just thinking of the platitudes to do with recession and so on, but the prevalence of such things as the 'bad' movie cult, where audiences go to laugh at and feel superior to a given art form.

STOPPARD: It's a form of decadence.

GOLLOB: Audiences so hungry for confirmation that they cannot afford imaginatively to step out to appreciate a 'new' *Rosencrantz*. I think a 'new' *Travesties* would be slammed—slammed because of a contraction of what the imagination of the theatre-going public is willing to concede.

STOPPARD: Do you really think that's true?

GOLLOB: Look at 1980, so far . . .

ROPER: Well, let's say that the seventies were filled with young writers writing socialist realism, partly because of audiences, though you can find audiences for anything, but because theatres such as the Warehouse and the Royal Court have been sponsoring that kind of thing.

STOPPARD: But, you see, Stuart Burge told me months ago that he'd love to get a play which upset that apple-cart completely, which upset one's preconceptions about what sort of play the Royal Court does. But you see, it's a vicious circle. The Royal Court does certain kinds of plays and therefore receives certain kinds of plays to do.

ROPER: Haven't you therefore categorised yourself as a non-Royal Court writer?

STOPPARD: Well, I sent them *Rosencrantz and Guildenstern* before it was ever done by anybody. But nothing happened.

GOLLOB: One of the Court's less successful efforts of the seventies—to try and hook up with what I was saying before—tried to use laughter as a double-edged weapon. I'm referring to Peter Barnes' play *Laughter*. Bernard Levin once said of you that you could write a play about Auschwitz and he would laugh.

STOPPARD: I don't think I could actually, or would wish to.

GOLLOB: In fact it's an amazing thing to say, but Barnes seems to have picked up the glove, so to speak, making a play where he goes into Auschwitz to try and point out how we use laughter as an escape, at the same time trying to make us laugh.

STOPPARD: What do you think yourself?

GOLLOB: I don't think it worked.

STOPPARD: Was it the principle at fault, or the execution?

GOLLOB: Well, let's put it this way. I think it was misconceived from the beginning. Comedy is based on incongruous juxtapositions, but this was a juxtaposition incapable of comedy.

STOPPARD: Yes, but the interesting thing about comedy is that it works in two completely different ways. It works by surprising people and by gratifying their expectations. I saw *The Hothouse* the other night and it was wonderful just to sit there and travel through the pause with the actor. There's no sense of being surprised, it's entirely to do with the inevitable gratification, when one says 'He's dead,' and you sort of wait, and wait, till the other says, 'Dead?'—it's marvellous, because there isn't any sort of wit involved in that exchange, but it's hilarious.

GOLLOB: Well isn't that 'bad'?

STOPPARD: No, no, the author is totally in control.

GOLLOB: By the time Barnes tried to make us laugh we'd already done too much of it. Something had happened to make us resistant to it, perhaps it was the jolt of '73-74 with the Yom Kippur War and the three-day week. And even though he was only trying to get us to laugh in order to force it back down our throats again, he failed because he couldn't get us motivated to do it in the first place.

STOPPARD: I'm just testing your general theory against experience. I'm not sure it holds up. It may be that people would have laughed in 1968 at **that** play, whereas they wouldn't in 1978. But people's willingness to laugh is something else . . . I'm just trying to think whether I feel differently about comedy.

GOLLOB: Good—as that is what I in my prolix way am trying to find out.

STOPPARD: Well, it's hard to be sure, but I don't think so. I think like a lot of writers I've got a cheap side and an expensive side. I mean rather like a musician might stop composing for a few days to do a jingle for 'Katomeat' because he thinks it's fun. And I honestly can't believe that because of something that happened to the world or to England I'll never write a 50-minute rompy farce for Ed Berman. I think I'd do it with as much pleasure as ten years ago.

But on the other side of the coin I think that you **are** onto something, that perhaps there is something in recent history which makes me feel that a play of more substance and less frivolity is more likely than the converse. I'm expressing this so carefully and so formally in order to try and get it right for myself. But one of the artificial—I nearly said false— things about being interviewed is that one pretends to have coherent ideas about oneself in order to gratify the expectations of the interviewer. But this isn't visible at all in the practice of writing a play, which is intimate and more to do with the next ninety seconds than the last nine years.

ROPER: Assuming you'd just written this 50-minute comedy, do you feel no political or moral ineptitude?

STOPPARD: That I can categorically answer to: none whatever. If I only wrote 50-minute farces, and you were to ask did I feel any sense of failure, the answer would be yes. But I don't think that anything that has happened in the world compromises the acceptability of the entertainment.

ROPER: You choose to live and work without this focus, then.

STOPPARD: Well, not all plays are written because of a gut need to write about factor X. In common with all professional writers one is asked whether one would like to do certain things . . . the BBC asks you if you'd like to adapt *Three Men in a Boat* and you don't think, 'These are not the times.' You say, 'Yeah, it's one of my favourite books, I'd love to have a crack at that.' And you do it. When it's a thing like that you're more a craftsman than an artist. I think it's right to take pride in one's craftmanship as much as one's originality.

GOLLOB: Somebody once said—I think Griffiths in *Comedians*—that comedy is essentially conservative, even reactionary.

STOPPARD: What an extraordinary thing to say! Is it?

ROPER: I think it is. Comedy is grounded in a kind of fellow-feeling, a sharing of feeling about society that reinforces those feelings and militates against change.

STOPPARD: That's very bright.

GOLLOB: It needs to be pessimistic about the outcome of change or innovation.

ROPER: It reinforces stasis, it makes you feel secure in what you are.

STOPPARD: Well, think of Tom Lehrer, does he reinforce shared values between performer and audience?

ROPER: Well, perhaps there's . . .

GOLLOB: *(interrupting)* I think he does!

ROPER: . . . a difference between comedy and strong satire.

STOPPARD: Well, I think you've got your knife out again to cut your sausage to suit you. If I said to you (and if we hadn't had this conversation) that comedy is a radical force, it wouldn't strike you immediately as being nonsense, one could make a case for it as much as you could for its being reactionary.

ROPER: You could, but if you were trying to make a serious point, you'd embarrass your audience. You embarrass them by trying to make them laugh at Auschwitz.

GOLLOB: Which is what Barnes did.

STOPPARD: But then is it still comedy?

GOLLOB: Quite . . . but if comedy contained a kind of constitutional inertia and were in some way resistant to change, could it be said that in your comic writing you regard man as not being perfectible, and that change should be resisted?

STOPPARD: Nothing could be further from the truth. First of all . . . the desire to reach perfection and the conviction that it is unattainable are compatible instincts. I think perfection is unattainable because it means different things to different people, but the need to make things better is constant and important. Otherwise you're into a sort of nihilism . . . You ring a bell with me somewhere . . . I think in that Tynan article. Somehow he got it wrong. Something I said made him conclude that I was somehow a writer who was not part of an effort to perfect society, some sort of striving for perfectibility. When I read it I thought, 'My God, how can he've got it so **wrong**?' Did you connect that with comedy in some way?

GOLLOB: Yes, I did. Let's look at *Night and Day* where the character Wagner comes in for a lot of sarcastic, comic roughing up. I too am a foreigner here, which perhaps made me feel sensitive or suspicious about the way this was happening. I began to identify not only with Wagner as a foreigner but also as someone associated with another kind of intrusion— the intrusion of unions into the area of 'free speech' and also as the intrusion

14

of a man who uses language in a certain way, not to mention a man who doesn't play the game according to the rules of cricket. Contrast this with Milne, so obviously public school background, the right sort of background which leads one to have the right sort of fundamental moral assumptions, closer to your heart, I felt, than Wagner. I saw the latter as a kind of usurper.

STOPPARD: My feelings about Wagner in particular and about journalism are rather ambivalent, but I admire Wagner rather a lot as a character. I would admire him if he existed. I admire good professionals. I'm a bit of a journalism groupie anyway. I think journalism is what Milne says it is, the last line of defence in this country. And surrounding this approbation is the knowledge that a great deal of journalism is despised and rightly so. I mean there is a lot of abuse in the mouths of other characters, particularly the woman. And she speaks for me as well. Nobody can have a cut and dried good/bad attitude towards Wagner or journalism because there are things to be said on different sides. She's a prejudiced observer with her own experience.

GOLLOB: You don't feel her voice is somehow more privileged by the fact that she's given two roles in the play, the other being this internal voice which can speak 'out' from behind the social mask.

STOPPARD: I didn't intend her to be privileged because of that. In fact I would have thought that—if there is such a person—the average watcher of this play would find that Milne carries more conviction than Ruth. Ruth has got a gift for sarcastic abuse, but what Milne says is true. I mean it is true: with a free press everything is correctible, however imperfect things are they are correctible if people know they're going on. If we don't know they're going on, it's concealable: true. I believe it to be a true statement. Milne has my prejudice if you like. Somehow unconsciously, I wanted him to be known to be speaking the truth.

GOLLOB: But he gets killed, though, doesn't he.

STOPPARD: That's what happens in myth. That in a sense confirms—not directly, but in some psychological way—the truth which he becomes a martyr to.

GOLLOB: But no, I mean, it depends on the treatment. Take a Christian sort of truth, like the kind you are taking, which is true in a sense essentially **because** it cannot survive—

STOPPARD: (*interrupting*) The play won't bear that sort of profundity, you see . . . you can follow that line of thought and it would be there in parallel with *Night and Day* and my experience of writing it, but because the play didn't spring from that kind of profound thought it's not that relevant to it. The press is a **real thing**, you know, papers are **real things** which you can **read**. And you like some of it and think it's important, and some of it you think is despicable. What one is trying to say is that a lot of it is hardly defensible but it's the price you pay for the part that matters. And that's all there is to it . . . Though there are other matters, as I said, I admire Wagner as a person because he takes his job seriously and is good at it and isn't a hack.

15

GOLLOB: I think there is a certain kind of typification going on in the way he is contrasted with Milne.

STOPPARD: Indeed, yes.

GOLLOB: Milne is a greenhorn, wet behind the ears, because he **believes** in his truth, and one isn't supposed to believe in things nowadays. We may admire him for having the courage of his convictions, but we ourselves tend to Wagner's more sceptical distance, tempered by experience. It seems to me that there is a kind of contrast going on between the ideal and the real, between innocence and experience. Ruth and Wagner are the critique revolving around this idealistic nucleus, as if in your thinking the very notion of freedom had an idealistic, even Kantian core.

STOPPARD: Yes, that's true.

GOLLOB: Hasn't it? I mean this notion one encounters in *Professional Foul* about human truths being self-evident things, *a priori* data one reflexively assumes to exist.

STOPPARD: Yes, yes.

GOLLOB: Now what I find so baffling is this: How does one reconcile this . . . this **idealism** with an opposite but more characteristic feature of your writing, which is the **relativism** of everything . . .

ROPER: (*interrupting*) I would've jumped back to the previous question where you said you felt that everything was going to be a striving for the better. As a philosophical construct, yes, but you have to accept that everything is polarized: Margaret Thatcher's better isn't Jim Callaghan's better. Isn't it your responsibility—if one is a writer—to acknowledge that?

STOPPARD: It's not, you see. It's not my responsibility as a writer. What I am interested in (you were talking about Kantian ideals and so on) is in what Margaret Thatcher and Jim Callaghan have **in common** which is not shared by . . . Hitler or Attila the Hun. At the ideal centre there is a way of behaving towards people which is good and a way which is bad . . . and alongside that different theories about attaining the common good—in other words, Callaghan and Thatcher each have different economic theories each designed literally to achieve the maximum general good for everybody. In other words, what you are talking about is merely a disagreement about tactic. But a play like *Professional Foul* is nothing to do with that, it's nothing to do with that at all. It's to do with the morality between individuals. I'm finding it hard to keep little boys out of my plays—my four sons aged between 5 and 14 may or may not be relevant—but something which has preoccupied me for a long time is the desire to simplify questions and take the sophistication out. A fairly simple question about morality, if debated by highly sophisticated people, can lead to almost any conclusion.

GOLLOB: Can you expand on that?

STOPPARD: Let me try. If somebody came out of East Germany through the gate in the wall and wished to communicate the idea that life inside this wall was admirable or indeed platonically good, he'd have a reasonable chance of succeeding in this if he were addressing himself to a sophisticated person. But if you tried to do this to a child, he'd blow it to smithereens. A child would say, 'But the wall is there to keep people **in**, so there must be some reason why people want to get out.'

There's a childlike truth about it. If it was good, people wouldn't want to leave. If people didn't want to leave, you wouldn't need to build a wall to keep them in. 'There's something wrong with what you are saying Professor!'

GOLLOB: I hope this doesn't make you feel I'm sophisticated but a child's logic cuts two ways. Throughout thousands of years we have been telling children on one hand that they are only children and so 'what do you know?' while on the other hand we have celebrated some kind of superhuman capacity to perceive *a priori* truths, untainted by tempering experience.

ROPER: And surely the position of the writer is **on** the wall, looking at both sides.

STOPPARD: Looping back over three sides of tape I can say that in the last few years I haven't been writing about questions whose answers I believe to be ambivalent. In *Every Good Boy* and *Professional Foul,* the author's position isn't ambiguous. Where the double-act comes into its own is in the tactical dispute between Margaret Thatcher and Jim Callaghan.

GOLLOB: Not Joseph and Benn?

STOPPARD: All I know is that I want to live in a country where that dispute can take place, and not where it's forbidden.

GOLLOB: Good, well, just to start rounding things up, is there anything you can tell us about new writing, about where you're moving to, or even where we're moving to?

STOPPARD: Well, the latter I wouldn't wish to, because I'd be busking. I don't see enough or read enough to have a proper acquaintance with what's happening or with what might happen next. As for myself, in the last three years I've written too much—more than I would comfortably wish to write . . . the only thing which I am presently committed to doing and which I am looking forward to doing is an adaptation from an Austrian play by Nestroy. Nestroy believe it or not is the man who wrote the original play which ended up as *Hello Dolly!* via Thornton Wilder.

ROPER: And do you refer to that as an adaptation or a version?

STOPPARD: It'll be much more a version than the Schnitzler. [*Undiscovered Country*].

GOLLOB: We often talk about waves and generations on the British drama scene. With whom, or on which would you like best to be seen surfing?

STOPPARD: I just think of myself as one of the people who came after the beginning. I mean, when I was on a newspaper in Bristol and Tynan was on the Observer, Osborne and Arden and Wesker and Pinter were I suppose the four best-known English playwrights, other than the pre-war generation. I just think of myself as one of the people who followed after that . . .

Tom Stoppard

WITHDRAWING WITH STYLE FROM THE CHAOS
Excerpts from a profile of Tom Stoppard
Kenneth Tynan*

During the nineteen-thirties there lived in Zlin—a town in Czechoslovakia
that is now known as Gottwaldov—a middle-class physician named Eugene
Straussler who worked for a famous shoe company. Either he or his wife
(nobody seems quite sure which) had at least one parent of Jewish descent.
In any case, Dr. Straussler sired two sons, of whom the younger, Thomas,
was born on July 3, 1937. Two years later, on the eve of the Nazi invasion
of their homeland, the Strausslers left for Singapore, where they settled
until 1942. The boys and their mother then moved to India. Dr. Straussler
stayed behind to face the Japanese occupation. He died in a Japanese air-raid,
or in a prisoner-of-war camp, or on a Japanese prison-ship torpedoed by the
British (nobody seems quite sure which). In 1946, his widow married a
Major in the British Army, who brought the family back with him to England.
The two Straussler scions assumed their stepfather's surname, which was
Stoppard. Thomas, who claims to have spoken only Czech until the age of
three, or possibly five-and-a-half (he doesn't seem quite sure which), grew
up to become, by the early nineteen-seventies, one of the two or three
most prosperous and ubiquitously adulated playwrights at present bearing
a British passport. (The other contenders are Harold Pinter, who probably
has the edge in adulation, and Peter Shaffer, the author of *Equus*, whose
strong point is prosperity.) There is no perfectly rational explanation for
any of this. It is simply true . . .

Tom Stoppard doesn't know

Stoppard often puts me in mind of a number in *Beyond the Fringe,*
the classic English revue of the sixties, in which Alan Bennett, as an
unctuous clergyman, preached a sermon on the text 'Behold, Esau my
brother is an hairy man, and I am a *smooth* man.' The line accurately
reflects the split in English drama which took place during (and has persisted
since) this period. On one side were the hairy men—heated, embattled,

*Reprinted by permission; © 1977 The New Yorker Magazine, Inc. Now published in
Show People by Kenneth Tynan; pub. Weidenfeld & Nicholson; £8.95 cb.

socially committed playwrights, like John Osborne, John Arden, and Arnold Wesker, who had come out fighting in the late fifties. On the other side were the smooth men—cool, apolitical, stylists, like Harold Pinter, the late Joe Orton, Christopher Hampton (*The Philanthropist*), Alan Ayckborn (*The Norman Conquests*), Simon Gray (*Otherwise Engaged*) and Stoppard. Stoppard once told an interviewer from the London weekly Time Out, 'I used to feel out on a limb, because when I started to write you were a shit if you weren't writing about Vietnam or housing. Now I have no compunction about that . . . *The Importance of Being Earnest* is important, but it says nothing about anything.' He once said that his favourite line in modern English drama came from *The Philanthropist*: 'I'm a man of no convictions— at least I *think* I am.' In *Lord Malquist and Mr. Moon* (1966), Stoppard's only novel to.date, Mr. Moon seems to speak for his author when he says, 'I distrust attitudes because they claim to have appropriated the whole truth, and pose as absolutes. And I distrust the opposite attitude for the same reason.' Lord Malquist, who conducts his life on the principle that the eighteenth century has not yet ended, asserts that all battles are discredited. 'I stand aloof,' he declares, 'contributing nothing except my example.' In an article for the London Sunday Times, in 1968, Stoppard said, 'Some writers write because they burn with a cause which they further by writing about it. I burn with no causes. I cannot say that I write with any social objective. One writes because one loves writing, really.' On another occasion, he defined the quality that distinguished him from many of his contemporaries as 'an absolute lack of certainty about almost anything.'

For Stoppard art is a game within a game—the larger game being life itself, an absurd mosaic of incidents and accidents in which (as Beckett, whom he venerates, says in the aptly entitled *Endgame*) 'something is taking its course.' We cannot know what the something is or whither it is leading us; and it is therefore impermissible for art, a mere derivative of life, to claim anything as presumptuous as a moral purpose or a social function. Since 1963, when the first professional performance of a script by Stoppard was given, he has written one novel, four full-length plays, one mini-play (*Dirty Linen*) that was cheekily passed off as a full-length entertainment, five one-acters for the stage, and ten pieces for radio or television. Thus far, only one of his performed works (*Jumpers*, to my mind his masterpiece, which was first produced in 1972) could be safely accused of having a moral or political message*; but the critics are always sniffing for ulterior motives—so diligently that Stoppard felt it necessary to announce in 1974, 'I think that in future I must stop compromising my plays with this whiff of social application. They must be entirely untouched by any suspicion of usefulness. I should have the courage of my lack of convictions.' In an interview he said he saw no reason that art should not concern itself with social and political history, but added that he found it 'deeply embarassing . . . when, because art takes notice of something important, it's claimed that the art is important. It's not.'

*In 1977, Tynan had not yet seen *Night and Day.*

Hating to be pinned down, politely declining to be associated with the opinions expressed by his characters, he has often remarked, 'I write plays because dialogue is the most respectable way of contradicting myself.' (Many of his apparent impromptus are worked out beforehand. Himself a one-time journalist, he makes a habit of anticipating questions and prefabricating effective replies. Indeed, such was his assurance of eventual success that he was doing this long before anyone ever interviewed him. When he read the printed result of his first conversation with the press, he said he found it 'very déjà vu.' Clive James, the Australian critic and satirist now working in London, has rightly described him as a 'dream interviewee, talking in eerily quotable sentences whose English has the faintly extraterritorial perfection of a Conrad or a Nabokov.')

Philosophically, you can see the early Stoppard at his purest in *Lord Malquist and Mr. Moon,* which sold only four hundred and eighty-one copies in 1966, when it was published. Malquist says:

> Nothing is the history of the world viewed from a suitable distance. Revolution is a trivial shift in the emphasis of suffering: the capacity for self-indulgence changes hands. But the world does not alter its shape or its course. The seasons are inexorable, the elements constant. Against such vast immutability the human struggle takes place on the same scale as the insect movements in the grass, and carnage in the streets is no more than the spider's sucked husk of a fly on a dusty window-sill.

Later, he adds, 'since we cannot hope for order, let us withdraw with style from the chaos.' When Moon, his biographer, a professed anarchist, attacks Malquist's anti-humanism on the ground that, whatever he may say, the world is made up of 'all *people,* isn't it?' Malquist scoffs:

> What an extraordinary idea. People are not the world, they are merely a recent and transitory product of it. The world is ten million years old. If you think of that period condensed into one year beginning on the first of January, then people do not make their appearance in it until the thirty-first of December; or to be more precise, in the last forty seconds of that day.
> Such trivial latecomers sound barely worth saving.

Though Stoppard would doubtless deny it, these pronouncements of Malquist have a ring of authority which suggests the author speaking. They reflect a world view of extreme pessimism and therefore conservatism. The pessimist is necessarily conservative. Maintaining, as he does, that mankind is inherently and immutably flawed, he must always be indifferent or hostile to proposals for improving human life by means of social or political change. The radical, by contrast, is fundamentally an optimist, embracing change because he holds that human nature is perfectible. The Malquist attitude, whatever its virtues, is hardly conducive to idealism. I recall a conversation with Derek Marlowe about Stoppard's private beliefs. 'I don't think,' Marlowe said, 'there's anything he would go to the guillotine for.' I found the choice of instrument revealing. We associate the guillotine with the decapitation of aristocrats. Marlowe instinctively identified Stoppard with the nobility rather than the mob—with reaction rather than revolution.

21

Into the arena of commitment?

There are signs, however, that history has lately been forcing Stoppard into the arena of commitment. Shortly after I wrote the above entry in my journal, he sent me a typescript of his most recent work. Commissioned by André Previn, who conducts the London Symphony Orchestra, it is called *Every Good Boy Deserves Favour*–a mnemonic phrase familiar to students of music, since the initial letters of the words represent, in ascending order, the notes signified by the black lines of the treble clef. Involving six actors (their dialogue interspersed with musical contributions from Mr. Previn's big band), it had its world première in July 1977 at the Royal Festival Hall, London. It started out in Stoppard's mind as a play about a Florida grapefruit millionaire, but his works have a way of changing their themes as soon as he sits down at his typewriter. The present setting is a Russian mental home for political dissidents, where the main job of the staff is to persuade the inmates that they are in fact insane. What follows is a characteristic exchange between a recalcitrant prisoner named Alexander and the therapist who is assigned to him:

> PSYCHIATRIST: The idea that all the people locked up in mental hospitals are sane whilst the people walking about outside are all mad is merely a literary cliché, put about by the people who should be locked up. I assure you there's not much in it. Taken as a whole, the sane are out there and the sick are in here. For example, *you* are in here because you have delusions that sane people are put in mental hospitals.
> ALEXANDER: But I *am* in a mental hospital.
> PSYCHIATRIST: That's what I said.

Alexander, of course, refuses to curry Favour by being a Good Boy. Beneath its layers of Stoppardian irony, the play (oratorio? melo-drama?) is a point-blank attack on the way in which Soviet law is perverted to stifle dissent. In the script I read, Alexander declares, at a moment of crisis, 'There are truths to be shown, and our only strength is personal example.' Stoppard, however, had crossed this line out, perhaps being reluctant to put his name to a platitude, no matter how true or relevant it might be. Simplicity of thought–in this piece, as elsewhere in his work–quite often underlies complexity of style. *E.G.B.D.F.* rests on the assumption that the difference between good and evil is obvious to any reasonable human being. What else does Stoppard believe in? For one thing, I would guess, the intrinsic merits of individualism; for another, a universe in which everything is relative yet in which moral absolutes exist; for a third, the probability that this paradox can be resolved only if we accept the posulate of a presiding deity. In 1973, during a public discussion of his plays at the church of St. Mary Le Bow in London, he told his interlocutor, the Rev. Joseph McCulloch:

> The whole of science can be said, by a theologian, to be operating within a larger framework. In other words, the higher we penetrate into space and the deeper we penetrate into the atom, all it shows to a theologian is that God has been gravely underestimated.

Nietzsche once said that convictions were prisons–a remark that the younger Stoppard would surely have applauded. I shall try to chart the route that has led Stoppard, the quondam apostle of detachment, to the convictions he now proclaims, and to his loathing for the strictly unmetaphorical prisons in which so many people he respects are at present confined . . .

An apostle of detachment

His career as a playwright began in 1960, when he wrote a one-act piece *The Gamblers*, which he described to me in a recent letter as *'Waiting for Godot* in the death cell–prisoner and jailer–I'm sure you can imagine the rest.' (It was staged in 1962 by Bristol University undergraduates and has never been revived.) Later in 1960, he spent three months writing his first full-length play, *A Walk on the Water*. It was so weightily influenced by Arthur Miller and by Rolbert Bolt's *Flowering Cherry* that he has come to refer to it as *Flowering Death of a Salesman*. He said in 1974 that, although he thought it worked pretty well on stage, 'it's actually phoney because it's a play written about other people's characters–they're only real because I've seen them in other people's plays.' A few years afterwards, indulging in his hobby of self-contradiction, he told a group of drama students, 'What I like to do is take a stereotype and betray it, rather than create an original character. I never try to invent characters. All my best characters are clichés.' This is Stoppard at his most typical, laying a smoke-screen to confuse and ambush his critics. Run the above statements together and you get something like this: 'It's wrong to borrow other writer's characters, but it's all right as long as they're clichés.' *A Walk on the Water* is about George Riley, a congenital self-deceiver who declares roughly once a week that he's going to achieve independance by leaving home and making his fortune as an inventor. Never having won more bread than can be measured in grams, he's entirely dependant–for food, shelter, and pocket money–on his wife and their teenage daughter, both of whom are wearily aware that, however bravely he trumpets his fantasies of self-sufficiency in the local pub, he is sure to be back for dinner. For all his dottiness (among his inventions are a pipe that will stay perpetually lit provided it is smoked upside down, and a revolutionary bottle-oppener for which, unfortunately, no matching bottle-top exists), Riley has what Stoppard describes as a 'tattered dignity'. This attribute will recur in many Stoppard heroes, who have nothing to pit against the hostility of society and the indifference of the cosmos except their obstinate conviction that individuality is sacrosanct. C.W.E. Bigsby says, in a perceptive booklet he wrote on Stoppard for the British Council:

> While it is clear that none of his characters control their own destiny . . .
> it is equally obvious that their unsinkable quality, their irrepressible
> vitality and eccentric persistence, constitute what Stoppard feels to be
> an authentic response to existence.

The first performance of *A Walk on the Water* (and the first professional production of any Stoppard play) was given on British commercial television in 1963. Considerably rewritten, and retitled *Enter A Free Man*, it was staged in the West End five years later when *Rosencrantz and Guildenstern* had established Stoppard's reputation. Both versions of the text are indebted not only to Miller and Bolt but to N.F. Simpson (the whimsical author of *One Way Pendulum*, a gravely surreal farce that contains a character whose ambition is to train a team of speak-your-weight machines to sing the 'Hallelujah Chorus'), and both pay respectful homage to P.G. Wodehouse and the British music hall comedy.

Wherever the 1968 text differs from the original, the changes are for the better, as witness the addition of Riley's crowning fancy–a device that supplies indoor rain for indoor plants. From Stoppard's deletions, however, we learn something crucial about the nature and the limitations of his talent.

'Tom cares more about the details of writing than anyone else I know,' Derek Marlowe told me. 'He's startled by the smallest minutiae of life. He'll rush out of a room to make a note about a phrase he's just heard or a line that's just occurred to him. But the grand events, the highs and lows of human behaviour, he sees with a sort of aloof, omniscient amusement. The world doesn't impinge on his work, and you'd think after reading his plays that no emotional experience had ever impinged on his world. For one thing, he can't create convincing women. His female characters are somewhere between playmates and amanuenses. He simply doesn't understand them. He has a dual personality, like the author of *Alice in Wonderland*. His public self is Charles Dodgson—he loves dons, philosophers, theorists of all kinds, and he's fascinated by the language they use. But his private self is Lewis Carroll–reclusive, intimidated by women, unnerved by emotion.'

Geoffrey Reeves agrees with this analysis: 'However abstract Beckett may seem, he always gives you a gut reaction. But Tom hasn't yet made a real emotional statement.'

Not long ago, I asked Stoppard what he thought of Marlowe's charge that his plays failed to convey genuine emotion. He reflected for a while and then replied: 'That criticism is always being presented to me as if it were a membrane that I must somehow break through in order to grow up. Well, I don't see any special virtue in making my private emotions the quarry for the statue I'm carving. I can do that kind of writing but it tends to go off, like fruit. I don't like it very much even when it works. I think that sort of truth-telling writing is as big a lie as the deliberate fantasy I construct. It's based on the fallacy of naturalism. There is a direct line of descent from the naturalistic theatre which leads you straight down to the dregs of bad theatre, bad thinking and bad feeling. At the other end of the scale I dislike Abstract Expressionism even more than I dislike naturalism. But you asked me about expressing emotion. Let me put the best possible light on my inhibitions and say that I'm waiting until I can do it well.' And what of Marlowe's comment that he didn't understand women? 'If Derek had said that I don't understand *people*, it would have made more sense.'

Taking a shine to boot

To revert to chronology: In 1960, the text of *A Walk on the Water* landed on the desk of Kenneth Ewing, the managing director of a newly-formed script agency, which now represents such writers as Michael Frayn, Charles Wood, Adrian Mitchell, and Anthony (*Sleuth*) Shaffer. Ewing sent Stoppard an encomiastic letter; the two men lunched in London; and Ewing has ever since been Stoppard's agent. 'When I first met him, he had just given up his regular work as a journalist in Bristol, and he was broke,' Ewing says. 'But I noticed that even then he always travelled by taxi, never by bus. It was as if he knew that his time would come.' In 1962, Stoppard heard that a new magazine called Scene was about to be launched in London; he applied for a job on the staff and was offered, to his amazement, the post of drama critic, which he instantly accepted. He then left Bristol for good and took an apartment in Notting Hill, a dingy West London residential area. Derek Marlowe lived in the same dilapidated house. 'Tom wrote short stories and smoked to excess, and always worked at night,' Marlowe recalls. 'Every evening he would lay out a row of matches and say "Tonight I shall write twelve matches"–meaning as much as he could churn out on twelve cigarettes.' Scene made its début early in 1963. Virulently trendy in tone and signally lacking in funds, it set out to cover the whole of show business. In seven months (after which the money ran out and Scene was no longer heard from), Stoppard reviewed a hundred and thirty-two shows. Years later, in a sentence that combines verbal and moral fastidiousness in a peculiarly Stoppardian way, he explained why he thought himself a bad critic: 'I never had the moral character to pan a friend or, rather, I had the moral character never to pan a friend.'

Since the magazine was ludicrously understaffed, he filled its pages with dozens of pseudonymous pieces, most of which he signed 'William Boot'. The name derives from Evelyn Waugh's novel *Scoop*, in which William Boot is the nature columnist of a national newspaper who, owing to a spectacular misunderstanding, finds himself shipped off to cover a civil war in Africa. (As things turn out, he handles the assignment rather well.) Boot took root in Stoppard's imagination, and soon began to crop up in his plays, often allied to or contrasted with a complementary character called Moon. As a double-act, they bring to mind Lenin's famous division of the world into 'who' and 'whom'–those who do and those to whom it is done. In Stoppard's words, 'Moon is a person to whom things happen. Boot is rather more aggressive.' Early in 1964, BBC radio presented two short Stoppard plays entitled *The Dissolution of Dominic Boot* and *M is for Moon Among Other Things*. The leading characters in *The Real Inspector Hound* (1968) are named Birdboot and Moon. A propos of the eponymous heroes of *Rosencrantz and Guildenstern* the English critic Robert Cushman has rightly said:

> Rosencrantz, being eager, well-meaning, and consistently oppressed or
> embarrassed by every situation in which he finds himself, is clearly a

Moon; Guildenstern, equally oppressed though less embarrassed and taking refuge in displays of intellectual superiority is as obviously a Boot.

Cushman once asked Stoppard why so many of his characters were called Moon and Boot. Stoppard replied crisply that he couldn't help it if that was what their names turned out to be. 'I'm a Moon, myself,' he went on. 'Confusingly, I used the name Boot, from Evelyn Waugh, as a pseudonym in journalism, but that was because Waugh's Boot is really a Moon too.' Having thus befogged his interviewer, he added a wry etymological touch. 'This is beginning to sound lunatic,' he said.

In 1964, a cobbler sticking to his last, Stoppard wrote a 90-minute TV play called *This Way Out with Samuel Boot*, which he equipped with a *pair* of Boots, who represent diametrically opposed attitudes towards material possessions. Samuel Boot, a fortyish man of Evangelical fervour, preaches the total rejection of property. Jonathan, his younger brother, is a compulsive hoarder of objects, unable to resist mail order catalogues, who fills his home with items bought on credit which are constantly being repossessed, since he never keeps up the payments. ('It's like Christmas in a thieves' kitchen,' Samuel cries, surveying a room stacked with vacuum cleaners, goggles, filing cabinets, miners' helmets, boomerangs, knitting machines, miniature Japanese trees and other oddments.) At one point, a salesman comes to deliver a hearing aid for a week's free trial. Having fitted the device into Jonathan's ear, he shouts into the box, 'There! that's better, isn't it?' 'You don't have to shout,' says Jonathan sharply, 'I'm not deaf.' He demands to know who told the salesman that he suffered from this infirmity.

SALESMAN: It was an assumption.
JONATHAN: If I told you I'd got a wooden leg, would you assume I was one-legged?
SALESMAN: Yes.
JONATHAN: Well, I have. And you may have noticed I'm wearing skis. You seem to be making a lot of nasty assumptions here. You think I'm a deaf cripple.

This reductio ad absurdum is pure Stoppard. An unreasonable man uses rational arguments to convince a reasonable man that he (the latter) is irrational. The salesman flees in panic, but Jonathan still has the hearing aid. Though both brothers are Boots by name, Samuel turns out to be a Moon by nature. He ends up defeated by his own innocence. When he claims to have found an exit from the commercial rat race, Jonathan brutally demolishes his dream:

There's no out. You're in it, so you might as well fit. It's the way it is. Economics. All this stuff I've got . . . people have been paid to make it, drive it to the warehouse, advertise it, sell it to me, write to me about it, and take it away again. They get paid, and some of them buy a carpet with the money. (He has just had a carpet repossessed.) That's the way of it and you are in it. There's no way out with Samuel Boot.

Jonathan has a vast collection of trading stamps. Samuel steals them and holds a public meeting at which he proposes to give them away. He's mobbed and killed by a crowd of rapacious housewives. 'He died of people,' says one of his disciples, a young deserter from the army. 'They trod on him.' To this, Jonathan replies, 'That's what it is about people. Turn round and they'll tread on you. Or steal your property.' The deserter delivers Samuel's epitaph:

> He was a silly old man, and being dead doesn't change that. But for a minute . . . his daft old crusade, like he said, it had a kind of dignity.

Whereupon he picks up as a souvenir of Jonathan's acquisitive way of life, a newly delivered vacuum cleaner. Rising to the defence of property, Jonathan shoots him dead with a mail-order harpoon gun.

Samuel Boot is patchily brilliant, an uneasy blend of absurdist comedy and radical melodrama. I have dwelt on it because (a) it is the last Stoppard play with a message (i.e. property is theft) that could be described as leftist, and (b) it is one of the few Stoppard scripts that has never been performed in any medium. Kenneth Ewing offered it to a London commercial TV company and took Stoppard with him to hear the verdict. It was negative. 'Stick to theatre,' he advised his dejected client on the way back. 'Your work can't be contained on television.' Then Ewing's thoughts moved to Shakespeare, and, for no reason that he can now recall, he brought up a notion he had long cherished about *Hamlet*. Quoting the speech in which Claudius sends Hamlet to England with a sealed message (borne by Rosencrantz and Guildenstern) enjoining the ruler of that country to cut off Hamlet's head, Ewing said that in his opinion the King of England at the time of their arrival might well have been King Lear. And, if so, did they find him raving mad at Dover? Stoppard's spirits rose, and by the time Ewing dropped him off at his home, he had come up with a tentative title, *Rosencrantz and Guildenstern at the Court of King Lear*. A seed had clearly been planted. It pleases Ewing to reflect that agents are not necessarily un-creative.

A scent of Saunders

Summing up his impressions of Stoppard . . . James Saunders says, 'Diffident on the surface, utterly unworried underneath. He's extremely cautious about being thought too serious. I've heard him quote Auden's famous remark to the effect that no poet's work ever saved anyone from a concentration camp. Well that may be true, but it's terrible to *admit* that it's true. After all, the writer's job is constantly to redefine the role of the individual: what can he do? what *should* he do? And also to redefine the role of society: how can it be changed? how *should* it be changed? As a playwright, I live between these two responsibilities. But Tom; Tom just plays safe. He enjoys being nice and he likes to be liked. He resists commitment of any kind, he hides the ultimate expression of his deepest concerns. He's basically a displaced person. Therefore, he doesn't want to stick his neck out. He feels grateful to

Britain, because he sees himself as a guest here and that makes it hard for him to criticise Britain. Probably the most damaging thing you could say about him is that he's made no enemies.' Since working together in Berlin, Stoppard's star has risen while Saunders' has tended to decline. I asked Saunders how this had affected their relationship. He smiled, and quoted a well-known British dramatist who had once told him, 'Whenever I read a rave review of a young playwright in the Sunday papers, it spoils my whole day.' He continued, 'When Tom first became famous, he gave a series of expensive lunches at the Café Royal to keep in touch with his old pals. I thought that was pretty ostentatious behaviour. Meeting him nowadays, I do feel a sort of cutoff.' He made a gesture like a portcullis descending. 'I don't think that he's overrated as much as that many other writers are underrated. He has distracted attention from people who have an equal right to it.'

Czech mates

When *Rosencrantz and Guildenstern Are Dead* had its London triumph (1967) Vaclav Havel was thirty years of age, just nine months older than Stoppard. He wore smart but conservative clothes, being a dandy in the classic rather than romantic mode. Of less than average height, he had the incipient portliness of the gourmet. His hair was trimmed short, and this gave him a somewhat bullet-shaped silhouette. He both walked and talked with purposeful briskness and elegance. He drove around Prague (where he was born on October 5, 1936) in a dashing little Renault, bought with the royalties from his plays–for in 1967 Havel was the leading Czechoslovakian playwright, and the only one to have achieved an international reputation since Karel Capek wrote *R.U.R.* and (with his brother Josef) *The Insect Play* between the wars. Havel's family connections were far grander than Stoppard's. Vera Blackwell, a Czech emigrée who lives in London and translates Havel's work into English, has said that 'if Czechoslovakia had remained primarily a capitalist society Vaclav Havel would be today just about the richest young man in the country.' One of his uncles was a millionaire who owned, apart from vasts amounts of real estate and a number of hotels, the Barrandov studios, in Prague, which are the headquarters of the Czech film industry. All this was lost in the Communist takeover of 1948, and during the dark period of Stalinist rigour that followed, Havel's upper-class background prevented him from receiving any full-time education above grade-school level. Instead, he took a menial job in a chemical laboratory, spending most of his off-duty hours at evening classes, where he studied science. In 1954, he began two years of military service, after which he made repeated attempts to enter Prague University. All his applications were turned down. His next move was to offer himself for any theatrical work that was going. He found what he was looking for in the mid-sixties, when he was appointed Dramaturg (i.e. literary manager, a post that in Europe quite often means not only play selector and script editor but house playwright as well) at the

Balustrade Theatre, which was Prague's principal showcase for avant-garde drama.

We nowadays tend to assume that the great thaw in Czech Socialism began and ended with the libertarian reforms carried out by Alexander Dubček's regime in the so-called Prague Spring of 1968. By that time, artistic freedom had in fact been blooming for several ebullient years: a period that saw the emergence of film-makers like Milos Forman, Ivan Passer, Jan Nemec, and Jan Kadar; of theatrical directors like Otomar Krejca and Jan Grossman (who ran the Balustrade); and of a whole school of young dramatists, at whose head Vaclav Havel swiftly established himself. In one sense, he was a traditional Czech writer. Using a technique that derived from Kafka, Capek and countless Central European authors before them, he expressed his view of the world in non-realistic parables. His plays were distorting mirrors in which one recognized the truth. Stoppard belongs in precisely the same tradition, of which there is no Anglo-Saxon equivalent. Moreover, Havel shares Stoppard's passion for fantastic word juggling. Some critics have glibly assigned both writers to the grab-bag marked Theatre of the Absurd. But here the analogy falters, for Havel's absurdism is very different from Stoppard's. Vera Blackwell says:

> Havel does not protest against the absurdity of man's life vis-à-vis the meaning-less universe, but against the absurdity of the modern Frankenstein's monster: bureaucracy . . . The ultimate aim of Havel's plays . . . is the improvement of man's lot (. . .)

If Dubček's policies represented what Western journalists called 'Socialism with a human face,' Havel's work gave Absurdism a human face, together with a socially critical purpose.

Like Stoppard, he had his first play performed in 1963. Entitled *The Garden Party*, it was staged by Grossman at the Balustrade. The hero, Hugo Pludek, is a student whose consuming interest is playing chess against himself. 'Such a player,' says his mother sagely, 'will always stay in the game.' His parents, a solid bourgeois couple, base their values on a store-house of demented proverbs that they never tire of repeating: e.g., 'Not even a hag carries hemp seed to the attic alone,' 'He who fusses about a mosquito net can never hope to dance with a goat,' 'Not even the Hussars of Cologne would go to the woods without a clamp,' and—perhaps the most incontrovertible of all—'Stone walls do not an iron bar.' They worry about Hugo, since he shows no inclination to apply for work in the ruling bureaucracy. Under their pressure, he attends a garden party thrown by the Liquidation Office, where he poses as a bureaucrat so successfully that before long he is put in charge of liquidating the Liquidation Office. From a high-ranking member of the Inauguration Service—the opposite end of the scale from the Liquidation Office—he learns the Party line on intellectual dissent: 'We mustn't be afraid of contrary opinions. Everybody who's honestly interested in our common cause ought to have from one to three contrary opinions.' Eventually the authorities decide to liquidate the Inauguration Service, and the question arises: Who should inaugurate the process of liquidation–an inaugurator or a liquidator? Surely not the former, since how can anyone inaugurate his own liquidation? But equally it can't be the latter, because liquidators have not been trained to inaugurate. Either liquidators must be trained to inaugurate or vice-versa. But this poses a new question: Who is to do the training? At the end of the play, driven mad by living in a society in which all truths are relative and subject to overnight cancellation, Hugo feels his identity crumbling. He knows what is happening to him, but good bureaucrat that he now is, he cannot resist it. In the course of a hysterical tirade, he declares:

> Truth is just as complicated and multiform as everything else in the world–the magnet, the telephone, Impressionism, the magnet–and we are all a little bit what we were yesterday and a little bit what we are today: and also a little bit we're not these things. Anyway . . . some of us are more and some of us are more not; some only are, some are only, and some only are not; so that none of us entirely is, and at the same time each one of us is not entirely.

This was Absurdism with deep roots in contemporary anxieties. The play was an immediate hit in Prague, and went on to be performed in Austria, Switzerland, Sweden, Finland, Hungary, Yugoslavia, and West Germany.

Linguists for socialism

Authentic satire operates on the principle of the thermos flask: it contains heat without radiating it. Havel's second play, *The Memorandum* (1965) was a splendid example: burning convictions were implicit in a structure of ice-cold logic and glittering linguistic virtuosity. His target was the use of language to subvert individualism and enforce conformity. Josef Gross, the managing director of a huge but undefined state enterprise, grows unsettled when he discovers that, on orders from above, the existing vernacular is being replaced by a synthetic language called Ptydepe, uncontaminated by the ambiguities, imprecisions, and emotional vagaries of ordinary speech. Its aim is to abolish similarities between words by using the least probable combinations of letters, so that no word can conceivably be mistaken for any other. We learn from the Ptydepe instructor who has been assigned to Gross's organisation, 'The natural languages originated . . . spontaneously, uncontrollably, in other words, unscientifically, and their structure is thus, in a certain sense, dilettantish.' For purposes of official communication they are utterly unreliable. In Ptydepe, the more common the meaning, the shorter the word. The longest entry in the new dictionary has three hundred and nineteen letters and means 'wombat'. The shortest is 'f' and at present has no meaning since science has not yet determined which word or expression is in commonest use. The instructor lists several variations of the interjection, 'Boo' as it might be employed in a large company where one worker seeks to 'shambush' another. If the victim is in full view, unprepared for the impending ambush and threatened by a hidden colleague, 'Boo' is rendered by 'Gedynrelom'. If however the victim is *aware* of the danger, the correct cry is 'Osonfterte'–for which 'Eg gynd y trojadus' must be substituted if *both* parties are in full view and the encounter is meant only as a joke. If the 'sham-ambush' is seriously intended, the appropriate expression is 'Eg jeht kuz'. Jan Ballas, Gross's ambitious deputy, points out to his baffled boss that normal language is fraught with undesirable emotional undertones: 'Now tell me sincerely, has the word "mutarex" any such overtones for you? It hasn't, has it! You see! It is a paradox, but it is precisely the surface inhumanity of an artificial language that guarantees its truly human function!' Gross's problems are compounded by the fact that he has received an official memorandum in Ptydepe, but in order to get a Ptydepe text translated one must make an application in Ptydepe, which Gross does not speak. 'In other words,' he laments, 'the only way to know what is in one's memo is to know it already.' Ever willing to compromise (and this is Havel's underlying message), he does not complain when he loses his job to Ballas; and it is through no effort of his own that he regains it at the end. The authorities have observed that, as one of their spokesmen resentfully puts it, wherever Ptydepe has passed into common use, 'it has automatically begun to assume some of the characteristics of a natural language: various emotional overtones, imprecisions, ambiguities.' Therefore, Ptydepe is to be replaced by a new language, Chorukor, based on the principle not of abolishing but of intensifying the similarities between words. Gross, reinstated to spearhead the introduction of Chorukor, remains what he has never ceased to be: a time-serving organization man.

This small masterpiece of sustained irony was staged throughout Europe and at the Public Theatre, in New York, where it won the 1968 Village Voice award for the best foreign play of the Off Broadway season. In April of that year, Havel's next work, *The Increased Difficulty of Concentration*, opened in Prague. If the logical games and mental pyrotechnics of *The Memorandum* suggested analogies with Stoppard, there were aspects of the new piece which anticipated a play that Stoppard had not yet written, namely, *Jumpers*. Havel's central character is Dr. Huml, a social scientist engaged (like Professor Moore in *Jumpers*) in dictating a bumbling lecture on moral values which goes against the intellectual grain of his society. He is interrupted from time to time by a couple of technicians bearing an extremely disturbed and unreliable computer with which they propose to study his behaviour patterns. Here are some telescoped samples of Huml at work, with Blanka, his secretary:

> HUML: Where did we stop?
> BLANKA: (*reads*) 'Various people have at various times and in various circumstances various needs–'
> HUML: Ah yes! (*Begins to pace*)–and thus attach to various things various values–full stop. Therefore, it would be mistaken to set up a fixed scale of values–valid for all people in all circumstances at all times–full stop. This does not mean however, that in all of history there exist no values

common to the whole of mankind–full stop. If those values did not exist, mankind would not form a unified whole–full stop . . . Would you mind reading me the last sentence? . . . There exist situations–for example, in some Western countries–in which all the basic human needs have been satisfied, and still people are not happy. They experience feelings of depression, boredom, frustration, etc.–full stop. In these situations man begins to desire that which in fact he does not need at all–he simply persuades himself he has certain needs which he does not have–or he vaguely desires something which he cannot have and therefore cannot strive for–full stop. Hence, as soon as a man has satisfied one need–i.e. achieved happiness–another so far unsatisfied need is born in him, so that every happiness is always, simultaneously, a negation of happiness.

Can science help man to solve his problems? Not entirely, says Huml, because science can illuminate only that which is finite, whereas man 'contains the dimensions of infinity.' He continues: 'We may perhaps be able to explain man, but never to understand him . . . The fundamental key does not lie in his brain, but in his heart.'

Meanwhile, the computer has broken down, and emits a shrill bombardment of imbecile questions, endlessly repeated:

Which is your favourite tunnel? Are you fond of musical instruments? How many times a year do you air the square? Where did you bury the dog? Why didn't you pass it on? When did you lose the claim? Do you urinate in public, or just now and then?

On August 21, 1968, the Soviet Union, alarmed by the experiment in Free Socialism that was flowering in Czechoslovakia, invaded the country and imposed on it a neo-Stalinist regime. One of the first acts of the new government was to forbid all performances of Havel's plays.

Styles of chaos

By the summer of 1968, Stoppard had had his third London première within fourteen months. *Enter a Free Man*, which I've already discussed, had opened to mixed notices at the St. Martin's Theatre in March, and *The Real Inspector Hound*, to which I'll return later, had been more happily received (the Observer compared it to a Fabergé Easter egg) when it arrived at the Criterion Theatre in June, just two months before the Russian tanks rolled into Prague. *Rosencrantz and Guildenstern* remained a great drawing card in the repertory of the National Theatre. A couple of weeks before its first night, in 1967, I had written for the New Yorker a piece on the performing arts in Prague. In it I said that the new Czech theatre was 'focussing its attention not only on man vs. authority but on man vs. mortality,' and that 'the hero is forced to come to terms not merely with the transient compulsions of society but with the permanent fact of death.' Under liberal governments, I added, authors tend to concern themselves with 'the ultimate problem of dying as well as the immediate problems of living.' With the benefit of hindsight, I realize that every word of this might have been written about *Rosencrantz and Guildenstern*: it fitted perfectly into my group portrait of Czech drama.

'Prufrock and Beckett,' Stoppard has said, 'are the twin syringes of my diet, my arterial system.' But has anyone noticed another mainline injection? Consider: Rosencrantz and Guildenstern are unaccountably summoned to a mysterious castle where, between long periods of waiting, they receive cryptic instructions that eventually lead to their deaths. They die uncertain whether they are victims of chance or of fate. It seems to me undeniable that the world they inhabit owes its atmosphere and architecture to the master builder of such enigmatic fables–Franz Kafka, whose birthplace was Prague, and who wrote of just such a castle. Stoppard is nothing if not eclectic.

Oscar Wilde (a good fairy, in the elfin sense of the word, who has more than once waved an influential wand over the accouchement of a Stoppard work) supplies an apt quotation, from *de Profundis*:

> I know of nothing in all Drama more incomparable from the point of view of Art, or more suggestive in its subtlety of observation, than Shakespeare's Rosencrantz and Guildenstern. They are Hamlet's college friends. They have been his companions . . . At the moment when they come across him in the play he is staggering under the weight of a burden intolerable to one of his temperament . . . Of all this Guildenstern and Rosencrantz realise nothing.

Which they prove in the funniest speech of Stoppard's play, when, having been told to 'glean what afflicts' Hamlet, the two spies quiz each other about his state of mind and come up with the following conclusion:

> ROSENCRANTZ: To sum up: your father, whom you love, dies, you are his heir, you come back to find that hardly was the corpse cold before his young brother popped on to his throne and into his sheets, thereby offending both legal and natural practice. Now why exactly are you behaving in this extraordinary manner?

Wilde goes on:

> They are close to his secret and know nothing of it. Nor would there be any use in telling them. They are little cups that can hold so much and no more . . . They are types fixed for all time. To censure them would show a lack of appreciation. They are merely out of their sphere: that is all.

Despite its multiple sources, *Rosencrantz and Guildenstern* is a genuine original, one of a kind. As far as I know, it is the first play to use another play as its décor. The English critic C.E. Montague described *Hamlet* as 'a monstrous Gothic castle of a poem, full of baffled half-lights and glooms.' This is precisely the setting of *Rosencrantz and Guildenstern*: it takes place in the wings of the Shakespearean imagination. The actor-manager who meets the two travellers on the road to Elsinore says that in life every exit is 'an entrance somewhere else.' In Stoppard's play, every exit is an entrance somewhere else in *Hamlet*. Sometimes he writes like a poet:

> We cross our bridges when we come to them and burn them behind us, with nothing to show for our progress except a memory of the smell of smoke, and a presumption that once our eyes watered.

And at other times with fortune-cookie glibness:

Eternity is a terrible thought. I mean, where's it going to end?

But we are finally moved by the snuffing out of the brief candles he has lit. Tinged perhaps with sentimentality, an emotional commitment has nonetheless been made. To quote Clive James:

The mainspring is the perception–surely a compassionate one–that the fact of their deaths mattering so little to Hamlet was something that ought to have mattered to Shakespeare.

The Real Inspector Hound, which joined *Rosencrantz and Guildenstern* on the London playbills in June 1968, need not detain us long. It is a facetious puzzle that, like several of Stoppard's minor pieces, presents an apparently crazy series of events for which in the closing moments a rational explanation is provided. Two drama critics, Birdboot and Moon, are covering the première of a thriller, written in a broad parody of the style of Agatha Christie. At curtain rise, there is a male corpse onstage. Stoppard unconvincingly maintains that when the play was half finished he still didn't know the dead man's name or the murderer's identity. (How did he find out? 'There is a God,' Stoppard says when he is asked this question, 'and he looks after English playwrights.') Toward the end, the two critics implausibly leave their seats and join in the action. In the dénouement, Moon, who is the second-string critic for his paper, is killed onstage by the envious third-string critic, who, posing as an actor in the play within a play, has previously slain the first-string critic (the curtain-rise corpse) and rigged the evidence to frame Moon. People sometimes say that Stoppard, for all his brilliance, is fundamentally a leech, drawing the lifeblood of his work from the inventions of others. In *Rosencrantz and Guildenstern* he battens on Shakespeare, in *Inspector Hound* on Christie, in *Jumpers* on the logical positivists, in *Travesties* on Wilde, James Joyce and Lenin. The same charge has of course been levelled against other and greater writers; in 1592 for example, the playwright and pamphleteer Robert Greene accused Shakespeare of artistic thievery, calling him an 'upstart crow, beautified with our feathers.' Allegations of this kind do not ruffle Stoppard's feathers. 'I can't invent plots,' he once said. 'I've formed the habit of hanging my plays on other people's plots. It's a habit I'm trying to kick.'

Unravelling jumpers

During the four years that separate *Inspector Hound* from *Jumpers* the total of new work by Stoppard consisted of three one-acters and a short play for television. This apparent unproductiveness was due partly to distracting upheavals in his private life (the collapse of his first marriage, the cementing of his new relationship with Miriam) and partly to an ingrained habit of preparing for his major enterprises with the assiduity of an athlete training for the Olympics. Or, to use Derek Marlowe's simile: 'For Tom, writing a play is like sitting an examination. He spends ages on research, does all the necessary cramming, reads all the relevant books, and then gestates the results. Once he's passed the exam–with the public as well as the critics–he forgets all about it and moves on to the next subject.' Moreover, the second play is always a high hurdle. Although *Inspector Hound* came after *Rosencrantz and Guildenstern*, it didn't really count, being a lightweight diversion, staged in a commercial theatre. The real test, as Stoppard knew, would be his second play at the National.

Early in 1970, he told me, over lunch, that he had been reading the logical positivists with fascinated revulsion. He was unable to accept their view that because value judgements could not be empirically verified they were meaningless. Accordingly, he said, he was toying with the idea of a play whose entire first act would be a lecture in support of moral philosophy. This led us into a long debate on morality–specifically, on the difference between the Judaeo-Christian tradition (in which the creator of the universe also lays down its moral laws, so that the man who breaks them is also committing an offence against God) and the Oriental tradition represented by Zen Buddhism (in which morality is seen as a man-made convention quite distinct from God or cosmogony). Only with Stoppard or Vaclav Havel can I imagine having such a conversation about a play that was intended to be funny. A few days later, Stoppard sent me a letter in which he said that our chat had 'forced me to articulate certain ideas, to their immense hazard, which I suppose is useful,' and went on, 'All that skating around makes the ice look thin, but a sense of renewed endeavour prevails–more concerned with the dramatic possibilities than with the ideas, for it is a mistake to assume that plays are the end-products of ideas (which would be limiting): the ideas are the end-products of the plays.'

Jumpers turned out to be something unique in theatre: a farce whose main purpose is to affirm the existence of God. Or, to put it less starkly, a farcical defence of transcendental moral values. At the same time it is an attack on pragmatic materialism as this is practised by a political party called the Radical Liberals, who embody Stoppard's vision of Socialism in action. George Moore, professor of moral philosophy, is Stoppard's hero, and it is not the least of his problems that he bears the same name as the world-famous English philosopher (d. 1958) who wrote *Principia Ethica*. George's role, one of the longest in the English comic repertoire, is devoted mainly to the composition of a hilarious, interminable, outrageously convoluted lecture designed to prove that moral absolutes exist–and closely analogous, as I've said, to the address dictated by Dr. Huml in Havel's *The Increased Difficulty of Concentration*. Theatrically, it disproves the philistine maxim that intellectual comedy can never produce belly laughs. George sums up his beliefs in a discussion with Archie:

> When I push *my* convictions to absurdity, *I* arrive at God ... All I know is

that I think that I know that nothing can be created out of nothing, that
m.y moral conscience is different from the rules of my tribe, and that
there is more in me than meets the microscope—and because of *that* I'm
lumbered with this incredible, indescribably and definitely shifty *God*,
the trump card of atheism.

He dismisses Archie's supporters as 'simplistic score-settlers.' George versus
Archie is Stoppard's dazzling dramatization of one of the classic battles of
our time. Cyril Connoly gives a more dispassionate account of the same
conflict in *The Unquiet Grave*, his semi-autobiographical book of
confessions and aphorisms:

> The two errors: We can either have a spiritual or a materialist view of life.
> If we believe in the spirit then we make an assumption which permits a whole
> chain of them, down to a belief in fairies, witches, astrology, black magic,
> ghosts and treasure-divining . . . On the other hand, a completely materialistic
> view leads to its own excesses, such as a belief in Behaviourism, in the economic
> basis of art, in the social foundation of ethics, and the biological nature of
> psychology, in fact to the justification of expediency and therefore ultimately
> to the Ends-Means fallacy of which our civilization is perishing . . .

In that great debate there is no question where Stoppard stands. He votes
for the spirit—although he did not state his position in the first person
until June 1977, when, in the course of a book review, he defined himself
as a supporter of 'Western liberal democracy, favouring an intellectual elite
and a progressive middle class and based on a moral order derived from
Christian absolutes.' In this context, Geoffrey Reeves' opinion is worth
quoting:

> *Rosencrantz* is a beautiful piece of theatre, but *Jumpers* is *the* play, without
> any doubt. The ironic tone perfectly matches the absurd vision. It's far more
> than an exercise in wit; it ends up making a fierce statement. Not necessarily
> one that I would agree with—politically and philosophically. Tom and I have
> very little in common. But it's a measure of his brilliance that in the theatre
> I suspend rational judgement. He simply takes my breath away. People
> sometimes say he has a purely literary mind. That's not true of *Jumpers*. It
> uses the stage *as* a stage, not as an extension of TV or the novel.

The increased difficulty of expression

By 1972, the year of *Jumpers*, the voice of Vaclav Havel had been
efficiently stifled. The ban on Czech productions of his work had
remained in operation since 1969. Censorship had returned to the press
and the broadcasting stations as well as to the theatre and the cinema; and
in January, 1969, Gustav Husák (Dubček's successor) made an ominous
speech in which he said that the time had come to 'strengthen internal
discipline.' He issued a strong warning to those who held 'private meetings
in their apartments for inventing campaigns' against the regime. Havel and
Jan Nemec, the film director, at once sent a courageous telegram to
President Ludvik Svoboda, protesting against Husák's threats and predicting

(with melancholy accuracy) that the next step would be police interrogations and arrests. Later in 1969, Havel received an American foundation grant that would enable him to spend a year in the United States. The Czech government responded by confiscating his passport. Productions of his plays outside Czechoslovakia had been effectively forbidden, because the state literary agency, through which all foreign contracts had to be negotiated, refused to handle Havel's work, on the ground that it gave a distorted picture of Czech life. This meant that thenceforward there was no officially sanctioned way for anything by Havel to be performed anywhere in the world. The authorities, however, were far from satisfied. What irked them was that they could drum up no evidence on which to bring him to court. He had engaged in no anti-state activities, and nothing in his plays could be construed as seditious. They recognized in him a stubborn naysayer, a non-collaborator; but dumb insolence was not a criminal offence. One of the archetypes of Czech literature is the hero of Jaroslav Hašek's novel *The Good Soldier Schweik*, who drives his superior officers to distraction by practising passive resistance beneath a mask of pious conformity. Like many Czech dissidents before him, Havel had learned from Schweik's example.

He continued to write. In 1971, the first draft of his latest play, *Conspirators,* translated by Vera Blackwell, reached my desk at the National Theatre. It is set in an unnamed country, conceivably South American, where a corrupt dictatorship has just been overthrown and replaced by a cautious and indecisive democratic government. A group of five staunch patriots (including the chief of police and the head of the general staff) hear rumours of a conspiracy to reinstate the deposed tyrant, now living in exile. Feaful that the new regime may be too weak to prevent a coup, they plan a countercoup of their own. One of them says, 'In order to preserve democracy, we shall have to seize power ourselves.' Their plot necessitates the use of violence, but whenever they meet they learn that their opponents are preparing to commit acts of comparable, if not greater, ferocity. This compels them to devise even more blood-thirsty countermeasures. The process of escalation continues until we suddenly realize what is happening. The rumours they hear about the exiled conspirators are in fact quite accurate accounts of their own conspiracy–reported by a government spy in their midst and fed back to them by one of their own agents in the Secret Service. In other words, as Havel put it in a letter to me, 'they have been plotting to save the country from themselves.' He warned me not to suppose that because the play dealt with politics it was a political play:

'I am not trying either to condemn or defend this or that doctrine . . . What I am concerned with is the general problem of human behaviour in contemporary society. Politics merely provided me with a convenient platform . . . All the political arguments in the play have a certain plausibility, and in some circumstances they might even be valid . . . The point is that one cannot be sure. For truth is not only what is said: it depends on who says it and why. Truth is guaranteed only by the full weight of humanity behind it. Modern rationalism has led people to believe that what they call objective truth is a freely transferable commodity that can be appropriated by anyone. The results of this divorce between truth and human beings can be most graphically observed in politics.'

A travesty of Joyce's political beliefs

The hard polemic purpose of *Travesties* is to argue that art must be independent of the world of politics. Carr says to Tzara, 'My dear Tristan, to be an artist *at all* is like living in Switzerland during a world war.' Tzara is the target of Stoppard's loathing of the avant-garde. He is made to describe himself as the 'natural enemy of bourgeois art' (which Stoppard cherishes) and as 'the natural ally of the political left' (which Stoppard abhors.) By lending his support to the anti-bourgeois forces, Tzara has pledged himself to the destruction of art. At one point he rounds on Joyce and says:

> Your art has failed. You've turned literature into a religion and it's as dead as all the rest, it's an overripe corpse and you're cutting figures at the wake. It's too late for geniuses!

What's needed, the zealous Dadaist goes on, is vandalism and desecration. Having set up Tzara in the bowling alley, Stoppard proceeds to knock him down with a speech by Joyce, which was not in the original script (it was suggested by the director) but which Stoppard now regards as 'the most important . . . in the play.' Joyce begins by dismissing Tzara as 'an over-excited little man, with a need for self-expression far beyond the scope of your natural gifts.' This, he says, is not discreditable, but it does not make him an artist: 'An artist is the magician put among men to gratify-capriciously-their urge for immortality.' If the Trojan War had gone unrecorded in poetry, it would be forgotten by history. It is artists who have enriched us with its legends–above all, with the tale of 'Ulysses, the wanderer, the most human, the most complete of all heroes.' He continues, 'It is a theme so overwhelming that I am almost afraid to treat it. And yet I with my Dublin Odyssey will double that immortality, yes by God *there's* a corpse that will dance for some time yet and *leave the world precisely as it finds it.'*

So much for any pretensions that art might have to change, challenge, or criticize the world, or to modify, however marginally, our view of it. For that road can lead only to revolution, and revolution will mean the end of free speech, which is defined by Lenin, later in the play, as speech that is 'free from bourgeois anarchist individualism.' Stoppard's idol–the artist for art's sake, far above the squalid temptations of politics is, unequivocally, Joyce. The first act ends with Henry Carr recounting a dream in which he asked Joyce what he did in the Great War. "I wrote *Ulysses,*' he said. 'What did you do?"

The implication of all this–that Joyce was an apolitical dweller in an ivory tower–is, unfortunately, untrue. He was a professed socialist. And this is where Stoppard's annexation of the right to alter history in the cause of art begins to try one's patience. (A minor symptom of the same sin occurs when Carr says that Oscar Wilde was 'indifferent to politics'–a statement that will come as a surprise to readers of Wilde's propagandist handbook *The Soul of Man Under Socialism*.) In a recent essay in the New York Review of Books, Richard Ellmann has pointed out that Joyce's library in Trieste was full of works by leftist authors; that the culmination of his political hopes was the foundation of the Irish Free State; and that Leopold Bloom in Ulysses is a left-winger of long standing who annoys his wife by informing her that Christ was the first socialist. Moreover, Ellmann quotes a speech from the autobiographical first draft of *A Portrait of the Artist* in which Joyce addresses the people of the future with oratorical fervour:

> Man and woman, out of you comes the nation that is to come the lightening of your masses in travail, the competitive order is arrayed against itself, the aristocracies are supplanted, and amid the general paralysis of an insane society, *the confederate will* issues in action.

The phrase I've italicized can only mean, as Ellmann says, 'the will of like-minded revolutionaries.' It is all very well for Stoppard to claim that he has mingled 'scenes which are self-evidently documentary . . . with others which are just as evidently fantastical.' The trouble with his portrait of Joyce is that it is neither one thing nor the other, neither pure fantasy nor pure documentary, but is simply based on a false premise. When matters of high importance are being debated, it is not pedantic to object that the author has failed to do his homework . . .

Speaking up for the outspoken

Simple chronology may be the best way to set out the convergence that subsequently developed between the lives, and careers, of Stoppard and Vaclav Havel.

August, 1976: Stoppard addresses a rally in Trafalgar Square sponsored by the Committee Against Psychiatric Abuse, from which he joins a march to the Soviet Embassy. There he attempts to deliver a petition denouncing the use of mental homes as punishment camps for Russian dissidents. 'The chap at the door wouldn't accept it,' he told me afterwards, 'so we all went home.'

October 5, 1976: Havel celebrates his fortieth birthday at the converted farmhouse, ninety miles from Prague, where he and his wife live. The next day he is officially ordered to quit the place, on the ground, patently false, that it is unfit for human habitation.

January 11, 1977: *Dirty Linen* opens on Broadway to generally favourable reviews. Walter Kerr, in his Sunday column in the New York Times, sounds one of the few discordant notes:

> Intellectually restless as a hummingbird, and just as incapable of lighting anywhere, the playwright has a gift for making the randomness of his flights funny . . . Busy as Mr Stoppard's mind is, it is also lazy; he will settle for the

first thing that pops in his head . . . Wide-ranging as his antic interests are, delightful as his impish mismatches can occasionally be, his management of them is essentially slovenly.

January 14, 1977: Vaclav Havel is arrested in Prague and thrown into jail. The real, though unacknowledged, reason for his imprisonment is that he is one of the three designated spokesmen for a document called Charter 77, signed by over three hundred leading Czech writers and intellectuals, which urges the government to carry out its promises, made in the Helsinki accords of 1975, to respect human rights, especially those relating to free speech.

February 11, 1977: Stoppard has an article in the New York Times about the new wave of repression in Prague. It starts:

> Connoisseurs of totalitarian double-think will have noted that Charter 77, the Czechoslovakian document which calls attention to the absence in that country of various human rights beginning with the right of free expression, has been refused publication inside Czechoslovakia on the grounds that it is a wicked slander.

Of the three leading spokesmen for Charter 77, two were merely interrogated and released—Jírí Hájek, who had been Foreign Minister under Alexander Dubček in 1968, and Jan Patočka, an internationally respected philosopher. (Patočka, however, was later rearrested, and, after further questioning, suffered a heart attack and died in hospital.) Havel alone was charged under the subversion laws, which carry a maximum sentence of ten years. 'Clearly,' Stoppard says, 'the regime had decided, finally, and after years of persecution and harassment, to put the lid on Václav Havel.'

February 27, 1977: Stoppard travels to Moscow with a representative of Amnesty International and meets a number of the victimized Soviet non-conformists, in support of whom he writes a piece for the London Sunday Times.

May 20, 1977: After four months' imprisonment in a cell seven feet by twelve, which he shared with a burglar, Havel is released. The subversion indictment is dropped, but he must still face trial on a lesser charge, of damaging the name of the state abroad, for which the maximum prison term is three years. He agrees not to make 'any political statements' while this new case is sub judice. The state attempts to make it a condition of his release that he resign his position as spokesman for Charter 77. He rejects the offer. Once outside the prison gates, however, he unilaterally announces that, although he remains an impenitent supporter of Charter 77, he will relinquish the job of spokesman until his case has been settled in court. He returns, together with his wife, to the farmhouse from which they were evicted the previous fall.

June 18, 1977: By now, Stoppard has recognized in Havel his mirror image—a Czech artist who has undergone the pressures that Stoppard escaped when his parents took him into exile. After thirty-eight years' absence (and two weeks before his fortieth birthday) Stoppard goes back to his native land. He flies to Prague, then drives ninety miles north to Havel's home, where he meets his Doppelgänger for the first time. They spend five or six hours together, conversing mainly in English. Stoppard tells me later that some of the Marxist signatories of Charter 77 regard Havel primarily as a martyr with celebrity value, and didn't want him as their spokesman in the first place. 'But they didn't go to jail,' Stoppard adds. 'He did. He is a very brave man.'

Like Stoppard, Havel asks only to be allowed to work freely, without political surveillance. But that in itself is a political demand, and the man who makes it on his own behalf is morally bound to make it for others. Eleven years earlier, Stoppard's hero Lord Malquist said, undoubtedly echoing his author's views, 'Since we cannot hope for order, let us withdraw with style from the chaos.' Stoppard has moved from withdrawal to involvement. Some vestige of liberty may yet be reclaimed from the chaos, and if Stoppard has any hand in that salvage operation, we may be sure that it will be carried out with style.

The National Theatre production of Arthur Schnitzler's *Undiscovered Country* in a version by Tom Stoppard, which opened in the Olivier Theatre on 20 June 1979. Director Peter Wood, settings by William Dudley.
(Photograph by Donald Cooper)

Dorothy (Julie Covington) and Jumpers in the National Theatre production of *Jumpers* directed by Peter Wood.   (Photograph by Zoë Dominic)

JUMPERS: A HAPPY MARRIAGE?
Tim Brassell

Tom Stoppard is without question the dramatist of the moment. In recent years the acclaim so universally afforded to *Dirty Linen* at the Almost Free Theatre and subsequently at the Arts Theatre, to *Every Good Boy Deserves Favour,* his unusual enterprise for the Royal Shakespeare Company and the London Symphony Orchestra, and to *Professional Foul,* a play for BBC Television, has brought his name, his face and, most importantly, his work to the attention of millions of people, few of whom, one ventures to suggest, regularly patronise the theatre. Yet his present reputation is emphatically the fruit of his past achievements, which commenced in 1966 with the phenomenal success of *Rosencrantz and Guildenstern Are Dead,* first at the Edinburgh 'Fringe' Festival and subsequently in the National Theatre's repertoire at the Old Vic. He followed this with a number of shorter pieces—*Albert's Bridge* (for radio), *After Magritte* (like *Dirty Linen,* for Ed Berman's Inter-Action) and *The Real Inspector Hound*—which tended to further his reputation for comic and especially verbal virtuosity rather than consolidate his status as a dramatist of considerable weight. Then, at the Old Vic, on February 2nd 1972 came Stoppard's first full-length play in five years, giving audiences the legitimate successor to *Rosencrantz* and the chance to determine whether Stoppard might prove himself a dramatist of lasting importance. *Jumpers* proved precisely that.

Perhaps the distinction between the interim pieces and *Jumpers* sounds forced, but it is one that Stoppard himself was concerned to make during an interview conducted for *Theatre Quarterly* magazine in 1974:

> I find it confusing to talk about 'my plays' as though *Hound* and *Jumpers* were the same sort of thing . . . *Jumpers* is a serious play dealt with in the farcical terms which in *Hound* actually constitute the play.

At the same time he outlined his specific objective in the longer plays.

> What I try to do is to end up by contriving the perfect marriage between the play of ideas and farce or perhaps even high comedy.

Two critical commonplaces immediately suggest themselves; first, that authors are not necessarily the best authorities on their own work, and secondly, that comedies are not necessarily not-serious. But each of these has been rather overlooked in the critical reception afforded *Jumpers* and, to some extent, all of Stoppard's writing.

In terms of popular success the play soon proved as illustrious as its justly acclaimed predecessor. In 1976, *Jumpers* was reintroduced into the National Theatre's repertoire at its new home on the South Bank, having run for two seasons at the Old Vic in 1972 and 1973. Michael Horden recreated his marvellous playing of the central role of George while Julie Covington played his wife Dotty, the part formerly taken by Diana Rigg. The Evening Standard readers who had voted Stoppard the Most Promising Playwright of 1967 (the year in which *Rosencrantz* first played at the Old Vic) voted *Jumpers* the Best Play of 1973 and Financial Times critic B.A. Young echoed the opinion of almost all his fellow-reviewers when he wrote:

> I can't hope to do justice to the richness and sparkle of the evening's proceedings, as gay and original a farce as we have seen for years, but a farce for people who relish truly civilised wit.[1]

This is praise indeed, and one baulks before disagreeing with it. Anyone who saw Peter Wood's productions would probably agree that *Jumpers* was as 'gay' and 'sparkling' as one could wish. But is *Jumpers* a farce? Is any of Stoppard's work, in fact, merely farcical? And what is the distinction between a farce and in Stoppard's words—'a serious play dealt with in farcical terms'? Jonathan Bennet, writing about *Rosencrantz* and *Jumpers* in the magazine *Philosophy* followed the reviewers and called *Jumpers:* 'a mildly surrealistic farce . . .(which) lacks structure and lacks seriousness'.[2] John Weightman, reviewing the play in *Encounter,* went further, declaring 'According to my antennae, quite a few bits of this play have not been brought fully into intellectual or aesthetic focus.'[3] To describe a play as a farce is, by definition, to suggest that its essential, and perhaps its sole objective is to excite laughter. In *Rosencrantz,* Stoppard was less obviously concerned with exciting laughter and the play's curious and poignant blend of comic and serious writing was almost universally recognised—if rather less universally admired. On his own admission, Stoppard attempts a similar mix in *Jumpers,* and despite receiving the highest praise, the play is labelled a farce. Two possibilities present themselves: either there has been widespread misinterpretation of the play or Stoppard has not made his serious intentions sufficiently clear.

What, in fact, is the nature of these intentions? In the course of the *Theatre Quarterly* interview, Stoppard said:

> *Jumpers* obviously isn't a political act, nor is it a play about politics, nor is it a play about ideology . . . On the other hand, the play reflects my belief that all political acts have a moral basis to them and are meaningless without it.

> *Is that disputable?*

> Absolutely. For a start it goes against Marxist–Leninism in particular, and against all materialist philosophy . . . *Jumpers* was the first play in which I specifically set out to ask a question and try to answer it, or at any rate put the counter-question.[4]

His thinking clearly pivots upon the morality or immorality of philosophical and political creeds, an idea carried through to *Travesties,* on which he was working at the time the interview was conducted, and, more obviously, to *Professional Foul.* What is particularly striking here is the way in which the questioner blandly asks 'Is that disputable?' seemingly taking Stoppard's earnest point for granted. It is quite possible—and quite likely—that the critical response to *Jumpers* has by and large made a similar assumption, and, by failing to look sufficiently deeply at the treatment of this idea, has missed its crucial relevance to the 'play of ideas', the dialectic between 'question' and 'counter-question' that is such an integral part of Stoppard's conception.

The dialect of *Jumpers* may not be immediately apparent to those familiar with it as a play telling the story of a work-obsessed philosophy professor named George Moore (but unconnected with the famous philosopher of the same name) and his nervy wife, Dotty, a former cabaret star, whose lives are complicated by the shooting of one of a troupe of University gymnasts performing in their Mayfair flat. This occurs while the man is forming part of a human pyramid at a party Dotty is throwing to celebrate an election victory that has brought the Radical-Liberal party to power, and he is subsequently identified as the late Professor McFee, also of the Philosophy Department. In the wake of the murder, elements of the 'whodunnit', familiar to Stoppard enthusiasts from *The Real Inspector Hound* and *After Magritte,* are introduced as Dotty, who seems to have shot the 'jumper' herself, tries to dispose of the corpse in her lavishly-appointed bedroom. In this task she is aided by the University's Vice-Chancellor, Archie, who is in the habit of visiting her regularly and at all hours, and hindered by the arrival of Inspector Bones. During all this, her husband remains quite impervious to the goings-on and, with the disorganisation and impracticality traditionally the preserve of University professors, he continues to prepare a paper for an imminent symposium on the subject 'Man: good, bad or indifferent?' making use of an unlikely collection of study-aids that includes a bow and arrow, a pet hare and a tortoise. Eventually Dotty is rescued from the clutches of the law by the resourceful Archie, who gets rid of the body and the inspector and then proceeds to oppose George at the symposium as a late replacement for McFee. With their debate, presented in a distorted, dream-like form, the play ends.

It is only at this point, in the 'coda' symposium, that Stoppard's 'question' and 'counter-question' actually confront each other, although they do so without dialectical clarity, as if projected out of a private nightmare of George's. Nevertheless the nature of the rival philosophical systems that are being fought out there is made clear throughout the play as we watch and listen to George preparing his case; he is attempting to argue against the prevailing attitudes represented by Archie and McFee, which insist upon a materialistic, pragmatic view of man and the universe. To this end he sets out to defend a God in whom he can't altogether bring himself to believe to support his determined belief in the moral and aesthetic standards which he holds to be a necessary basis for civilised human activity. One of the main reasons that the 'coda' does not present this debate more directly is that the subject under debate there is effectively under debate throughout the play. Stoppard sets up George and Archie as the protagonists in a play of ideas by providing a constant interplay for and against the philosophy generally referred to as Logical Positivism. McFee and Archie are the zealous proponents of the philosophy, George the muddled but vehement opponent. (Even his servant, Crouch, is an enthusiastic amateur.) The debate between their positions spans the whole of *Jumpers,* neatly assimilating all the various strands of its plot into a subtle structural unity. For Stoppard is concerned not merely to conduct a theoretical debate, but to illuminate the Logical Positivist philosophy in action, with all the attendant consequences. To this end he presents the practical implications of the philosophy through a futuristic situation in which it has become philosophical orthodoxy, and Radical-Liberalism, its political arm, has just won a general election. The seemingly diverse elements of *Jumpers* represent the tragi-comic consequences of a Logical Positivist status quo and a world that is running mad as a result. In view of which, it is surprising that Doctor Bennett, a distinguished philosopher, should conclude his dismissive comments about the play with the assertion: 'there is nothing here that deserves the attention of philosophers.'[5] Like a number of drama critics, he treats the philosophical content of *Jumpers* as something not altogether integral to Stoppard's conception. In order to demonstrate just how integral I take it to be, it will first be expedient to sketch, in necessarily broad terms, the main tenets of Logical Positivism, and if this sounds improbable in the midst of a discussion of *Jumpers,* that further emphasises the play's unrecognised seriousness.

Logical Positivism originated in Vienna in the early 1920's where the Professor of Philosophy at the University, Moritz Schlick, and a group of like-minded colleagues who included leading mathematicians and scientists established the 'Vienna Circle'. Foremost among its members were Rudolph Carnap and Otto Neurath, and their fundamental stance is neatly summarised by Neurath's profession:

> All the representatives of the Circle are in agreement that 'philosophy' does not exist as a discipline, alongside of science, with propositions of its own; the body of scientific propositions exhausts the sum of all meaningful statements.[6]

The objective was thus to deprive philosophy of its traditional position of privileged independence, which the Circle considered obsolescent in the Twentieth Century, to clear all mystification from the field of philosophy and to rationalize it along strictly scientific lines. The intensity of the group's commitment to science can be identified from their use of such terminology as 'atomic facts', and the radicalism of their goal was matched only by their characteristically zealous single-mindedness in pursuit of it.

At the heart of the Vienna Circle's approach was the verification principle, which was an insistence that observability, either actual or possible, was a predicate of all knowledge that could be regarded as genuine. Strictly factual statements whose validity could be tested in practice were to be regarded as the only meaningful order of assertions. Thus 'truth' was directly equated with scientific verifiability, and all areas of investigation outside the category of factual assertion were not philosophical.

It was this dismissal of areas of enquiry recognised as the legitimate preserve of the philosopher by centuries of tradition that attracted often rabid hostility to Logical Positivism, especially after the Second World War, when its influence grew to the point at which it was practically the new orthodoxy in academic circles. Opponents insisted that this extreme empiricism was not only misguided but actually dangerous. They argued that man does not live merely on the materialistic level of scientific fact, and that examining the concepts of goodness and beauty, or speculating on the nature of God and the universe (all deprecated by Logical Positivists) were not merely legitimate areas of study but were vital to the conduct and content of living. To exclude all areas of metaphysical, ethical or aesthetic enquiry, and the consideration of absolute categories (such as Plato's 'Theory of Forms' or the Christian concept of sin) was considered a grave threat to the whole quality of life.

A representative and important critic of Logical Positivism in this country was C.E.M. Joad, whose book *A Critique of Logical Positivism* was published in 1950, a time when the influence and academic respectability of Logical Positivism was at its height. Joad is less anxious to defend metaphysics per se than to point out the implications of practical living on the basis of Logical Positivist assumptions. His particular target is A.J. Ayer's book *Language, Truth and Logic,* a handbook of Logical Positivist orthodoxy. To argue against what can be scientifically proven would be perverse, but Joad's argument is not against scientific method as such; it is rather against the exclusion of areas of thought and inquiry to which science cannot provide the answers. For, example, he describes Ayer's intractable position on God as being:

> neither atheist nor agnostic; it cuts deeper than either by assering that all talk about God, whether pro or anti, is twaddle.[7]

on the basis of Ayer's clinical and carefully-worded assertion that, to the Logical Positivist, 'all utterances about the nature of God are nonsensical.'[8] What is really at stake here is not belief in God as such, but the concept of a philosophy intractably rooted in materialism. Ayer's statement insists that **logical** talk about God is impossible because, if he exists, his existence is evidently of a metaphysical nature. One cannot quibble with the truth of this assertion, but one can certainly quibble with its implication, which is that one should not bother oneself with whether God exists or not. Joad defends the inscrutable, insisting that things that we cannot know for certain can be of very great importance, and that there can and **must** be a realm of philosophy beyond that rooted in what can be apprehended and verified by scientific means.

Ethnics is a particularly telling case in point. Because we cannot 'know' goodness in the sense in which we can 'know' that grass is green, the Logical Positivist concludes that we cannot really know it at all. Ayer declares that sentences

> which express moral judgements do not say anything. They are pure expressions of feeling and as such do not come under the category of truth and falsehood.[9]

The stringency of this insistence upon a materialistic notion of 'truth' is nowhere more evident than here. Ethics is obviously not a field that can be reduced to terms of logical consistency or inconsistency, or which can be based solely on observable facts. But if ethics are excluded from the field of truth, the total relativity that results is liable to render them almost insignificant. One does not have to look far to see that the character and structure of a society are built upon the shared ethics of individuals, and similarly that its man-made beauty is built upon shared aesthetics. The danger is that by reducing all value-judgements to 'expressions of feeling' one is effectively licensing immorality and ugliness, and Ayer's patronising caveat glosses over the problem:

> To say that moral judgements are not fact-stating is not to say that they are unimportant, or even that there cannot be arguments in their favour. But these arguments do not work in the way that logical or scientific arguments do.[10]

He makes no real concession here (for the primacy of 'logical or scientific arguments' is unimpaired) and instead gives the distinct impression of trying to have it both ways. As Joad says:

> The claim is that clarity of thought is so effectively promoted that when exhibited in the light of the logical positivist method of analysis and translation many, perhaps most, of the problems of philosophy disappear. And so, no doubt, they do. But they disappear not because they have been solved but because they are dismissed.[11]

What is fundamentally at issue, then, is whether its reduction of all philosophy to logical premises that can then be accepted or rejected effectively means that Logical Positivism put into practice would authorise the most solipsistic and pragmatic forms of conduct. This is the question which Joad's book and Stoppard's play both pose, and the two writers clearly share a belief that academic debate about philosophy does not take place in an irrelevant vacuum, and that trends in academic thought percolate into the social and cultural climates to affect the way that we all live and think. Thus Stoppard's aim is broadly that of Joad, who states at the outset of his *Critique:*

> I am concerned to enquire what effects are liable to be produced by Logical Positivism upon the minds of those who are brought into contact with it and to consider whether these are such as are desirable.[12]

Such an enquiry provides the implicit and unifying structure of *Jumpers:* it presents domestic, academic and even extra-terrestial situations where human values seem to be corroding and explores them as the direct and adverse consequences of materialistic habits of thought.

The central representative of Logical Positivist orthodoxy in *Jumpers*
is the University's Vice-Chancellor, Sir Archibald Jumper, a dandy of
seemingly innumerable talents in the fields of philosophy, law, medical
therapy, politics and gymnastics, to name just a few. His special interest
in encouraging gymnastics provides a pun on his own name—his students
are 'Jumpers' in two senses—as well as suggesting a continuation of the
ancient Greeks' mixture of recreational and intellectual pursuits. His
political interests naturally focus upon the Radical–Liberal party, which
gives his philosophy a political arm, and as one of the party's stalwarts,
he seems to be running the victory celebrations at Dotty's flat with
which the play opens. The Rad-Lib's success at the polls initiates a
regime committed to wholesale rationalisation of the nation and its
institutions, and we have several hints as to how they intend to pursue
their radicalism: among their earliest actions, for instance, is the
appointment of Sam Clegthorpe, the atheist Radical–Liberal spokesman
for agriculture, as Archbishop of Canterbury. His importance as the
party's only leader mentioned by name in *Jumpers* is reinforced when
he figures in the nightmarish 'coda' sequence. Before this, however,
George spots him from the window of his flat:

> Good God! I can actually see Clegthorpe marching along, attended by two
> chaplains in belted raincoats. (p. 38)

This 'rationalisation' of the church (like the railways!) establishes an
episcopal hierarchy more reminiscent of the mafia than the clergy.
Elsewhere, the military implications of the Radical-Liberals' success are
suggested when the couple hear jets flying low overhead:

> George: Oh yes, the Radical-Liberals . . . it seems in dubious taste . . .
>   soldiers . . . fighter-planes . . . After all, it was a general election,
>   not a *coup d'etat*.
> Dotty: It's funny you should say that.
> George: Why?
> Dotty: Archie says it was a coup d'etat not a general election. (p. 34)

'Archie says' is a recurrent phrase of Dotty's which serves to indicate both
the influence he has over her and the influence he has gained through
insinuating himself into as many disciplines as he can. This is not
dilletantism, but a power complex, and it is largely realised when the
Radical–Liberals win the election after a campaign centred on the philosophy
'No problem is insoluble given a big enough plastic bag' (p. 40)—a motto
which emphasises the narrow scope of 'problems' that Logical Positivists
are prepared to recognise. When Dotty is trying to dispose of the corpse
she shows her susceptibility to the philosophy by asking George, 'You
don't happen to have a large plastic bag, do you?' (p. 41) which seems
absurdly comic, but the joke rebounds when this turns out to be precisely
the manner in which Archie and his gymnasts do dispose of the problem!
Jumpers shows us the disturbing extent to which the Vice-Chancellor
practises precisely what he preaches, and his behaviour throughout the

49

play illustrates the moral limbo that opponents insist is a consequence of Logical Positivism's narrowing emphasis upon the practical aspects of rational behaviour.

A further example is demonstrated on the English moon expedition which Dotty watches on her bedroom television. There, with an ironic reversal of Oates' chivalry and self-sacrifice on the famous British Antarctic expedition of 1912, we see the astronaut-in-command, Captain Scott, fight with his subordinate officer Oates for a place in the capsule, after it has been damaged on landing. Scott originally figured in the coda in person, but Stoppard has deleted this from the published edition, leaving him as a symbol of Logical Positivism stretching the horizons of its deadening rationality right out into the universe. For what could be more rational than wanting to save your own neck, when the reward for practising abnegation is a slow and airless martyrdom on the surface of the moon? In such a situation the Logical Positivist can console himself in the knowledge that generosity and selflessness are merely emotional whims.

This sense of human behaviour overtaking established values is central to *Jumpers,* although it is established only indirectly, by such means as television newsreel, people passing and Dotty's digested snippets of Archie's opinions. The play itself, in fact, never moves outside the setting of George and Dotty's flat, which besides being dramatically convenient, also suggests something of man's alienation from political actuality. The action alternates between study and bedroom to focus in turn upon George's losing battle against his materialistic academic colleagues, Dotty's losing battle against her own nerves and, obliquely hinted at, their losing battle to keep their marriage afloat. But in Stoppard's comedy this last is a subject for humour rather than trauma, and it is the couple's individual roles which are of central importance. George's role is primarily bound up with his attempt to refute the rationality of the Logical Positivist case. Although he frequently (and comically) flounders, the integrity of his intentions ensures our sympathy for his efforts to prove that there is a source of meaning and values in the universe. His position is not that of the convinced Christian but of the determined humanist:

> If God exists, he certainly existed before religion. He is a philosopher's God, logically inferred from self-evident premises. That he should have been taken up by a glorified supporters' club is only a matter of psychological interest. (pp. 39-40).

Nevertheless George needs a Godhead to support his beliefs that values are not arbitrary and that science cannot exhaust truth. He tries to convince Dotty that reason alone cannot provide the touchstone of truth:

> The National Gallery is a monument to irrationality! Every concert hall is a monument to irrationality!–and so is a nicely kept garden, or a lover's favour, or a home for stray dogs! You stupid woman, if rationality were the criterion for things being allowed to exist, the world would be one gigantic field of soya beans! . . . The irrational, the emotional, the whimsical . . . these are the stamp of humanity which makes reason a civilising force! (p. 40).

50

Rationality is, however, the criterion of the uncivil Radical-Liberals in all things, and as George widens the argument to include aesthetics and art and love, the shortcomings of the criterion are magnified. But George nevertheless remains unable to translate his objections to Logical Positivism into the coherent alternative philosophy for which he is constantly searching.

His wife's fragile state has apparently sprung largely from the violent blow dealt to her sensibility when men first landed on the moon and quashed all her treasured romantic associations:

> They thought it was overwork or alcohol, but it was just those little grey men in goldfish bowls, clumping about in their lead boots on the television news; it was very interesting, but it certainly spoiled that Juney old moon; and much else besides . . . (p. 39)

Now Scott's behaviour takes the process a stage further, coinciding with the Radical-Liberal's victory to suggest the onward march of pragmatic standards of human conduct within the ever-onward march of materialism. Dotty's singing career came to an abrupt end with the rape of her 'spoony, Juney moon' and she remains highly strung throughout the play. Her breakdown seems representative of the human response to the removal of cherished irrational values such as those the moon and the church represented. We learn that rebellious Christians have stormed Lambeth Palace ('My chaplains had to use tear-gas to disperse them' (p. 84) the frantic Clegthorpe admits) but no-one can restore the moon's lost aura of romantic innocence.

Dotty's vulnerability in a world of fast-changing values estranges her from the intellectual George and leads her to an emotional dependence upon Archie. But she is not wholly won over to Logical Positivism, and we can see the idealistic and irrational inside her rebelling against the philosophy to which, under Archie's influence she pays lip-service:

> There's no question of things getting better. Things are one way or they are another way; 'better' is how we see them, Archie says . . . things and actions, you understand, can have any number of real and verifiable properties. But good and bad, better and worse, these are not the real properties of things, they are just expressions of our feelings about them. (p. 41)

It is precisely this tension between her nominal acceptance of the rational and her inward clinging to the irrational which produces her mental disorder, and from which her appeal as a character largely springs. The rupture of her fond and dreamy associations of the moon, derived from the songs whose cliches she can no longer manage to sing, becomes symbolic of the shattering demands constantly being made on us by the march of scientific progress. Yet Dotty's position, although unenviable, is in a sense a privileged one, showing the resilience of human sensibility to the implacable demands of reason and materialism. It is therefore appropriate that her neurosis should culminate in a vision of apocalyptic proportions:

> Well, it's all over now. Not only are we no longer the still centre of God's
> universe, we're not even uniquely graced by his footprint in man's image . . .
> and all our absolutes, the thou-shalts and thou-shalt-nots that seemed to be
> the very condition of our existence, how did they look to two moonmen with
> a single neck to save between them? Like the local customs of another place.
> When that thought drips through to the bottom, people won't just carry on.
> There is going to be such . . . breakage, such gnashing of unclean meats, such
> coveting of neighbours' oxen and knowing of neighbours' wives, such
> dishonourings of mothers and fathers, and bowing and scraping to images
> graven and incarnate, such killing of goldfish and maybe more—
> Because the truths that have been taken on trust, they've never had edges
> before, there was no vantage point to stand on and see where they stopped. (p. 75)

Dotty's 'vision' here is intuitive and heartfelt, expressing the 'logical' progression of science and philosophy that reduces men from God's beloved,
unique creation to just another scientific specimen in a global jar; Archie's
clipped question in response to this passionate torrent—'When did you first
become aware of these feelings?' (p. 75)—is especially ironic when one
considers that to the Logical Positivist all value-statements **are** simply
'expressions of feeling'.

Dotty's response provides her character with what is broadly required to
create the pun on her name; she simply fails to cope with the pressures of
the brave new reality and passes most of the play drifting about her bedroom
in a confused state. Her reaction to the new rationalism is matched by the
Christians who rebel against the government's anti-religious dictates, and
also, as Crouch tells George, by Dotty's apparent victim, McFee. The Professor
of Logic himself stumbled from the pinnacle of Logical Positivist orthodoxy
shortly before his death:

> It was the astronauts fighting on the Moon that finally turned him, sir. Henry,
> he said to me, Henry, I am giving philosophical respectability to a new
> pragmatism in public life, of which there have been many disturbing examples
> both here and on the moon. Duncan, I said, Duncan, don't let it get you down,
> have another can of beer. But he kept harking back to the first Captain Oates,
> out there in the Antarctic wastes, sacrificing his life to give his companions a
> slim chance of survival . . . Henry, he said, what made him do it?—out of the
> tent and into the jaws of the blizzard. If altruism is a possibility, he said, my
> argument is up a gum-tree . . . Duncan, I said, Duncan, don't you worry your
> head about all that. That astronaut yobbo is good for twenty years hard. Yes,
> he said, yes, **maybe**, but when he comes out, he's going to find he was only
> twenty years ahead of his time. I have seen the future, Henry, he said, and it's
> yellow. (p. 79/80)

McFee's apprehensive notion of 'giving philosophical respectability to a new
pragmatism' is the lynchpin of Stoppard's play of ideas. It serves to put
Dotty's apocalyptic vision into a more rational and accurate perspective—
one that is correspondingly more disturbing. By contrasting Scott on the
moon with Oates at the Antarctic it also stresses how the gulf between
bravery and unselfishness and cowardice and self-interest is left without
any kind of demarcation by the Logical Positivists' reduction of all value-

judgements to the interplay of relative emotions. As the Radical-Liberals with their yellow flags and the Jumpers with their yellow tracksuits attire themselves in the colour traditionally associated with cowardly behaviour, Stoppard draws out the obvious moral implications, emphasising them finally in McFee's horrified vision of a yellow future.

Within the play, McFee's retraction also isolates Archie as the sole dedicated adherent of Logical Positivism, and it is inevitably he who coolly steps in to oppose George in the 'coda' symposium. *Jumpers* seems to reveal only one breach in his clinical poise, only one pointer to any humane content in his life: his fondness for Dotty as he helps her out of the murder scrape, and administers skin therapy to alleviate her neurosis. But close examination casts doubt even on this. His dermatological experiments are an extension of his scientific personality, unemotional and serving perhaps as a wry reminder that, as Joad says, 'For logical positivists the world consists only of sensual facts.' (p. 63)—an appropriate pun in view of the constant ambiguity that Stoppard suggests in Archie's bedroom activities with Dotty. This is never resolved either way and we are left as much in the dark as George, but it is worth considering that Logical Positivists do recognise the animal, emotional side of men; they merely state that it is not susceptible to evaluative judgements! Alongside his professed 'medical' interest in her is his defence of her after Bones has found the corpse. Bones is prepared to be as lenient as he can, and his own values are not wholly unprejudiced— 'Show business is my main interest, closely followed by crime detection' (p. 46). But this is not sufficient for Archie:

Bones: My advice to you is, number one, get her lawyer over here—
Archie: That will not be necessary. I am Miss Moore's legal adviser.
Bones: Number two, completely off the record, get her off on expert evidence—nervous strain, appalling pressure, and one day—snap!—blackout, can't remember a thing. The other half is, get something on Mad Jock McFee, and if you don't get a Scottish judge, it'll be three years probation and the sympathy of the court.
Archie: That is most civil of you, Inspector, but a court appearance would be most embarrasing to my client and patient; and three years' probation is not an insignificant curtailment of a person's liberty.
Bones: For God's sake, man, we're talking about a murder charge.
Archie: You are. What I had in mind is that McFee, suffering from nervous strain brought on by the appalling pressure of overwork—for which I blame myself entirely—left here last night in a mood of deep depression, and wandered into the park, where he crawled into a large plastic bag and shot himself . . . (*Pause. Bones opens his mouth to speak*) . . . leaving this note . . . (Archie *produces it from his pocket*) . . . which was found in the bag together with his body by some gymnasts on an early morning keep-fit run. (*Pause. Bones opens his mouth to speak.*) Here is the coroner's certificate. (Archie *produces another note, which* Bones *takes from him.* Bones *reads it*)
Bones: Is this genuine?
Archie: Of course it's genuine. I'm a coroner, not a forger (p. 64/65)

Once again, Archie has wheedled his way into all the necessary spheres of influence, but where Bones' desire to aid Dotty clearly springs from his admiration and affection for her, Archie's seems to be based on the principle that corruption is all right provided that it works—which, a detractor might add, is a fairly Logical Positivist stance. Indeed, after offers of bribery and patronage fail, Archie is forced to resort to blackmail with Dotty fabricating a bogus cry of rape, in order to get rid of the Inspector. The very considerable wit with which Stoppard manages this scene does not in the least dimimish the exhibition in it of wholly amoral and unprincipled conduct.

For a murder has been committed; McFee is dead, and the 'whodunnit' elements in *Jumpers* are wholly integral to the interplay of ideas for and against Logical Positivism. The fact that it **looks** as if Dotty shot him leads all concerned, including the audience to assume that she has, but this is hardly proof, as we recall from Archie's indignation when George expresses doubt as to the medical nature of his activities in Dotty's bedroom: 'Well, what would it have *looked* like if it had *looked* as if I was making a dermatographical examination?' (p. 78). And indeed it **looks** as if Bones has tried to rape Dotty only because she has contrived, presumably at Archie's beck, to make it look like that. Perhaps, similarly, it has been **made** to look as if Dotty is guilty, for, as Archie says, 'The truth to us philosophers, Mr. Crouch, is always an interim judgement. We will never know for certain who did shoot McFee.' (p. 81).

Such a conclusion falls considerably short of satisfying both the inspector (who mistrusts philosophy anyway) and the whodunnit enthusiasts in Stoppard's audiences, however consistent it may seem with the facts, and with the stringent demands of the Vice-Chancellor's logical principles. However, the fact that this follows hard upon the revelation of McFee's despairing retraction and his intention of entering a monastery, circumscribes these closing words of Archie's with an extremely similar implication which could put a rather different interpretation upon his motives for trying to get Dotty off the hook. For in an earlier encounter with Bones the following dialogue occurred:

> Archie: With the possible exception of McFee's fellow gymnasts, anybody could have fired the shot, and anybody could have had a reason for doing so, including, incidentally, myself.
> Bones: And what might **your** motive be, sir?
> Archie: Who knows? Perhaps McFee, my faithful protege, had secretly turned against me, gone off the rails and decided that he was St. Paul to Moore's Messiah . . . McFee was the guardian and figurehead of philosophical orthodoxy, and if he threatened to start calling on his masters to return to the true path, then I'm afraid it would certainly have been an ice-pick in the back of the skull. (p. 63/64)

At that stage of the play the idea sounded ludicrous; it is, however, precisely what **did** happen to McFee, who told Crouch of his 'conversion'. The inspector has no way of knowing of this, but, shortly afterwards, Archie tests out George's knowledge of the previous night's events:

54

Archie: Oh he could be very violent, you know . . . In fact we had a furious
row last night–perhaps the Inspector had asked you about that . . . ˆ
George: No . . .
Archie: It was a purely trivial matter. He took offence at my description of
Edinburgh as the Reykjavik of the South. (p. 68/9)

Together these quotations comprise a strong case for believing that a violent
disagreement actually did take place between McFee and Archie when the
Vice-Chancellor discovered the nature of his protegé's recent apprehensions,
and that Archie responded in almost as murderous a manner as the one he
incautiously describes to Bones at a point when he thinks their quarrel
undiscovered.

These suspicions are further justified by the fact that when George
learns of the murder, Dotty says, casually, 'I thought Archie did it'
(throughout the play no-one has actually **asked** her if she did it!), and by
the manner of Clegthorpe's death in the coda. This, as I have said, is
presented as though it were a despairing private nightmare taking place
inside George's head, and in it his apprehensions about the moral behaviour
implicitly licensed by Logical Positivism are shown at their zenith as
Archie controls the symposium in neo-fascist style. (Interestingly, this
is one of Joad's stated concerns: that the moral vacuum created by the
attempted debasement of ethics is susceptible to fascist infiltration.) In
the coda we see the moral current moving inexorably towards solipsistic
self-interest, and even Clegthorpe, besieged by Christian rebels, draws back
from the abyss:

Clegthorpe: In my opinion the Government is going too fast.
Archie: Surely that is a matter best left to the Government?
Clegthrope: They were shouting 'Give us the blood of the lamb. Give us
the bread of the body of Christ'–
Archie: That's hardly a rational demand!
Clegthorpe: They won't go away! . . . Surely belief in man could find room
for man's beliefs? (p.84)

But the Radical-Liberals' 'belief in man' is a humanism steered rigidly along
Logical Positivist lines, and Clegthorpe is promptly executed, shot out of a
pyramid of Jumpers, just as McFee was. Archie rids himself of his 'turbulent
priest' by transforming the symposium into a trial, but this hardly offers a
solution to the problems posed by the irrational basis of Christian belief.
Once again, the problems are not being solved but dismissed.

This is Archie's method in all things, and it strongly suggests that the
status of the coda is not entirely subjective–a bizarre experience of
George's–but is designed to put beyond doubt our suspicions of Archie
that have accumulated at the end of the play proper. The audience alone
is in a position to make the logical deduction: that the help Archie gives
Dotty is designed to defray suspicion from himself.

George would have easily 'won' the symposium with his 'opponent'
taking his side. But Archie preserves the Logical Positivist case by
stepping into the gap, seemingly with impunity, and in between the

courtroom activity and Dotty's songs he does try to present his side's case in the discussion 'Man: Good, Bad or Indifferent?' His first speech is an incoherent (and Joycean) babble, that is extremely funny and earns him shattering applause (and scores of '9.7', '9.9' and '9.8') but hardly advances the Logical Positivist cause. After George's speech, however, he has the chance to defend himself, the only point in the play when the two philosophical positions come truly face to face. George's case rests on the value and importance of the non-scientific, non-verifiable content of life, but his struggle throughout the play to convincingly express this gets him nowhere until, in the coda, he attempts to outline the double standards he regards as necessarily implicit in Logical Positivism:

> A remarkable number of apparently intelligent people are baffled by the fact that a different group of apparently intelligent people profess to a knowledge of God when common sense tells **them**—the first group of apparently intelligent people—that knowledge is only a possibility in matters that can be demonstrated to be true or false, such as that the Bristol train leaves from Paddington. And yet these same apparently intelligent people, who in extreme cases will not even admit that the Bristol train left from Paddington yesterday . . . will, nevertheless, and without any sense of inconsistency, claim to **know** that life is better than death, that love is better than hate, and that the light shining through the east window of their bloody gymnasium is more beautiful than a rotting corpse! (p. 86/7)

However much this fails to assert non-logical positives, which is and always will be a major problem of philosophy, it at least presents a cogent illustration of the limitations of merely logical ones, and with some dexterity, suggests that the Logical Positivist is in practice forced to maintain fundamentally contradictory attitudes towards ethical and aesthetic standards.

In response, Archie puts forward a pragmatically optimistic but evasive and uncreditable defence:

> Do not despair—many are happy much of the time; more eat than starve, more are healthy than sick, more curable than dying; not so many dying as dead; and one of the thieves was saved. Hell's bells and all's well—half the world is at peace with itself, and so is the other half; Vast areas are unpolluted; millions of children grow up without suffering deprivation, and millions, while deprived, grow up without suffering cruelties, and millions, while deprived and cruelly treated none the less grow up . . . (p. 87)

The shortcomings of this glib and 'factual' account are as evident as the Beckettian influence on Stoppard's style here. But where Beckett hovers mercilessly on the edge of the holocaust, Stoppard steers us safely clear of the brink to suggest, by a negative implication, the immorality that **could** be logically acceptable to an order perpetrating the philosophy's rigid rationality: lack of respect for life, the pursuit of hate, equanimity in the face of deprivation and suffering, a chaos of values, stemming from the Logical Positivist's insistence that facts stand or fall by logical tests alone. Their evaluation is something with which he does not concern himself. In this manner, albeit within a comic framework, Stoppard shows the perversity of holding evaluation to be a matter of merely emotional significance, and suggests some of the deplorable values that the philosophy shields beneath a bogus façade of rose-tinted logic.

It should now be clear that the play's 'question' and 'counter-question' are of rather more than theoretical interest to its author. In broad terms, George is the play's hero and Stoppard's own mouthpiece. Archie is indicted as the representative of Logical Positivism and (as the streams of the 'whodunnit' puzzle and the play of ideas slowly converge) as the villain of the piece in two senses. The manner of Dotty's emotional recoil from the implications of Logical Positivism and its spheres of influence also provides a counterpart to her husband's intellectual repulsion. Yet even in the heart of some of the funniest sequences between the characters he creates in *Jumpers*, Stoppard rarely steps very far away from the relentless illumination of the ultimate consequences of an all-pervasive logicality. Here George is trying to explain McFee's position to Inspector Bones:

> George: The point is it allows him to conclude that telling lies is not **sinful** but simply anti-social.
> Bones: And murder?
> George: And murder, too, yes.
> Bones: He thinks there's nothing **wrong** with killing people?   .
> George: Well, put like that of course . . . But **philosophically** he doesn't think it's actually, inherently wrong in itself, no.
> Bones (*amazed*):   What kind of philosophy is that?
> George: Mainstream, I'd call it. Orthodox mainstream. (p. 48/9)

This, of course, is exactly what we see happen in the course of the play; it also demonstrates the position that Stoppard is concerned to put George in, so that within the ranks of Academe his role, ironically, is that of the sceptic. Archie's patronising regard for George is demonstrated when he refers to him as:

> our tame believer, pointed out to visitors in much the same spirit as we point out the magnificent stained glass in what is now the gymnasium.

Throughout, George is clearly regarded as the local eccentric. John Weightman has not perceived the irony of this when he endorses the description by calling him 'an eccentric who is trying to set back moral philosophy forty years',[13] for this is, of course, to **endorse** Archie's position. What Stoppard wants us to see in George is the norm distorted by his environment into the apparent eccentric. His efforts may seem as futile as Canute's, but his motives and beliefs are surely somewhat sounder. Yet within the world of ebbing values that Stoppard depicts, esteem for George's whole area of concern has been so far undermined that:

> Only the Chair of Divinity lies further beyond the salt, and that's been vacant for six months since the last occupant accepted a position as curate in a West Midland diocese.

The consequences of such a debasement of ethics are the running theme of the entire comedy.

In making a summary assessment of *Jumpers*, then, the pertinent question is whether the dramatic form that Stoppard has employed with such zest and, indeed, originality, makes his position and the serious elements of his concept sufficiently discernible? In a recent interview with André Previn, he declared:

> What seems to interest some people about the work I write, the question to ask about it apparently, is whether it's serious work compromised by frivolity or frivolous work redeemed by being serious.[14]

In a nutshell, we have here the 'problem' of *Jumpers*; for if frivolity gains the upper hand we do presumably have a mere farce, and if seriousness gains the upper hand the comedy risks being left behind by the play of ideas. But this kind of thinking in itself militates against taking *Jumpers* on the terms on which Stoppard offers it, with his self-professed aim of a 'marriage' between these two elements.

Dorothy (Julie Covington) and George (Michael Hordern) in the National Theatre production of *Jumpers*. (Photograph by Zoë Dominic)

To take the play as a farce is to see the farcical mechanics—the sexual ambiguity, the body swinging away from view as the bedroom door opens, George's bizarre appearance on the Inspector's arrival, foamed for a shave and carrying a tortoise and bow and arrow—in isolation, without recognizing the intellectual pattern by which Stoppard schematizes them. These techniques do, however, make a major contribution to the play's theatricality and entertainment-value, and it is hard to conceive how one could succeed in presenting a philosophical argument in the theatre, without resource to some such methods. Stoppard's objective is in some ways a Shavian concept, though one which Shaw never really achieved in practice, and if *Heartbreak House,* for instance, shows the comic elements being swamped by Shaw's earnestness, *Jumpers* shows the balance clearly tipping in the opposite direction—to the point at which the philosophical content of the play is in danger of becoming opaque. Where the play does succeed best is often in its smallest units where the two 'marriage' partners truly converge in wit of the very highest standard, simultaneously provoking laughter and thoughtfulness:

> George: Poor Duncan . . . I like to think he'll be there in spirit
> Archie: If only to make sure the materialistic argument is properly
> presented. (p.69)

Notes

1. *Financial Times* 3rd February 1972
2. 'Philosophy and Mr Stoppard', *Philosophy* Vol. 50, Jan. 1975, pp. 5,8
3. 'A Metaphysical Comedy', *Encounter,* Vol. 38, April 1972, p. 45
4. *Theatre Quarterly,* Vol. IV, No. 14, pp. 12, 16
5. 'Philosophy and Mr Stoppard', op. cit., p.8
6. 'Sociology and Physicalism', *Logical Positivism,* ed. Ayer; Allen & Unwin, 1959, p.282
7. *A Critique of Logical Positivism,* Gollancz, 1950, p. 31
8. Quoted, ibid, p. 116
9. Quoted, ibid, p. 115
10. *Logical Positivism,* op. cit., p.22
11. *A Critique of Logical Positivism,* op. cit., p.22
12. *A Critique of Logical Positivism,* op. cit., p.17
13. 'A Metaphysical Comedy', op. cit.
14. 'André Previn Meets . . . Tom Stoppard', broadcast on BBC 1

Hound (David Henry), Felicity (Nina Thomas), Cynthia (Cherith Mellor) in
The Real Inspector Hound at the Young Vic, June 1980.
(Photograph by Christopher Pearce)

DROPPING THE OTHER BOOT
or Getting Stoppard Out of Limbo
Dougald McMillan

His skill and intelligence are too impressive to ignore, yet in the view of influential critics Tom Stoppard has written no obvious masterpiece to confirm his lasting importance. He has, therefore, been assigned to the realm of the perpetually gifted but not yet accepted. In fact since *Rosencrantz and Guildenstern Are Dead* Tom Stoppard has been kept in limbo.

Criticism of Stoppard has been crystallized in a pattern of imagery which has kept critics from seeing his achievements. The pattern, by now almost obligatory, has three metaphors: light, movement and food. First, Stoppard's verbal wit and intellectual acuity is acknowledged in a metaphor of light: 'bright', 'brilliant', 'dazzling', 'glitter', 'sparkle', etc. Implied in these terms is a kind of ambiguity: the work is impressive but . . .

At this point the argument usually switches to metaphors of purposeless activity–motion without goal, stasis, games. Kenneth Tynan in his *New Yorker* 'Profile' speaks of a 'literary circus' in which characters 'jump through hoops'. *Travesties* is a triple-decker bus going nowhere. *The Real Inspector Hound* is a 'facetious puzzle.' Water Kerr calls Stoppard 'an intellectual hummingbird unable to light anywhere'. Ronald Hayman in the first full-length critical study refers to 'theatrical antics' which are only 'decoration for a drama which is essentially static'. Danniel Henniger in *The Wall Street Journal* calls Stoppard's characters 'Harlem globe trotters of the intellect passing around an argument'.

Sometimes the metaphor is expressed as confectioner's art. Tynan uses Stoppard's own phrase from *Jumpers*, accusing him of 'constructing a Gothic arch out of junket' in *Travesties* and cautions, 'Cake, as Marie Antionette discovered too late, is no substitute for bread.' Stanley Kauffman in his *Saturday Review* account of *Night and Day* (Feb. 2, 1980) compares Maggie Smith's performance to a 'cookie mold . . . pressing out sentences that can be wrapped, packaged and mailed overseas'. Kauffmann also expresses his doubts in terms of champagne, at first *Travesties* 'seemed to bubble' but 'It wasn't heading anywhere' and 'the bubbles flattened'. There are many other examples from other critics but these are typical.

These metaphors register two simultaneous but distinguishable reactions: first, that Stoppard himself is about no serious purpose, and second, that the plays fail to follow the recognizable patterns expected by the audience. Tynan's reaction to *Travesties* is the most fully articulated example of this objection:

> What it lacks is the sine qua non of theatre namely a narrative thrust that impels
> the characters, whether farcically or tragically or in any intermediate mode,
> toward a creditable state of crisis, anxiety or desperation.

Whether the objections are that Stoppard lacks serious purpose or that he
fails to satisfy the expectations of his audience, the result is the same. The
metaphors of bright light and purposeless activity or confections work
together to suggest both great promise and a failure to fulfil that promise.
Some critics like Hayman have waited expectantly for the play that will
finally prove Stoppard's lasting merit. Others, like Kauffmann and Robert
Brustein, have waited petulantly for a chance to declare definitively that
Stoppard's promise was illusory, but until recently critics have waited. With
Stoppard's shift to more directly political subject matter, his detractors,
using the same kinds of metaphor which have characterized earlier assessments,
have reached their verdict. Kauffmann in his review of *Night and Day* now
declares that the 'diamonds' were 'rhinestones' all along. Brustein in his
review of that play for the *New Republic* (5, 12 Jan 1980) pronounces that
Stoppard is:

> the author of very clever journalists. (. . .) He has insinuated himself into the
> affections of smart people like a heartworm, usurping whatever place might
> have been reserved there for genuine artists. He has used his considerable
> gifts in the service of a shell game conning the intelligentsia into finding him
> significant with a few philosophical reflections on a few intellectual themes.
>
> As a dramatist Stoppard is a dandy. His plays toy with difficult subjects, but
> they are essentially not very serious. They are pirouettes by a rather vain dancer
> who knows he can leap higher than anyone else but seems to have forgotten
> why.
>
> Whatever might be cogent in this material is obscured (Sic!) by an excess of
> verbal sparks and stylish posturing distracting us from the author's intentions
> to the author's manner.

These metaphors might be dismissed as harmless attempts to enliven otherwise
rather ordinary critical journalism if they did not form a consistent pattern
of evaluation which has become a substitute for extended examination of the
plays. These critical metaphors are examples of the fault they castigate: the
substitution of momentary, facile expression for serious purpose. They lead to
a self-confirming but false view of Stoppard. In the absence of careful, informed
reading of the plays, (as opposed to impressionistic reactions, plot summary,
self-congratulatory identification of sources, and often irrelevant biographical
anecdotes) the serious concerns and purposeful construction of Stoppard's
plays remain undefined and therefore unrecognized. The argument that they
do not exist is confirmed by default.

Ironically, the very sins of which he is accused are ones Stoppard has
attacked in his own plays. Already in *Rosencrantz and Guildenstern*, in an
image adumbrating those used by his critics and by himself in a more
developed form in *The Real Inspector Hound*, Stoppard has Rosencrantz
point out that, in the comic scenes with Polonius, Hamlet is not 'selling
toffy apples'—not offering easy satisfaction served up on a stick.

Drama has more intellectual substance. The substance of Stoppard's own drama and his achievement are already significant. He has used the play itself as an important vehicle of dramatic criticism. In doing so he has cleared the way for himself and others to write plays which are not dependent on reductive explanation of character and mechanistic denouement. In his own brand of farce he has developed the play of ideas into the drama of philosophical propositions.

Rosencrantz and Guildenstern Are Dead, The Real Inspector Hound, Jumpers, Artist Descending and *After Magritte* examine in their different ways the proposition that the drama of revealed motivation is dead. Rosencrantz and Guildenstern are dead partly because their ostensible function in the play is superfluous. Their stated role, to 'glean what afflicts' Hamlet, is like the conventional search on the part of the audience to understand psychological motivation. They have to 'find out what's the matter . . . it's a matter of asking the right questions and giving away as little as possible'. But, in fact, they are not successful: 'What a fine persecution' says Guildenstern, 'to be kept intrigued without ever quite being enlightened.'

In their search for motives they are preceded by Polonius as he 'discovers' the 'very cause' of Hamlet's madness. Polonius describes himself as one who 'hunts . . . the trail of policy.' The tracking of culprits is to become Stoppard's metaphor for the search for explanation of motivation and a neat denouement. Just after he is told by the players of Polonius' theory of 'unrequited love', Rosencrantz assumes for a moment the role of a sleuth, 'Nobody leaves the room—without a very good reason.' In his frustrated attempt to get answers from the other characters, he escalates to the pitch of a full scale police raid. 'All right, we know you're in there, come out talking.'

While Rosencrantz and Guildenstern stay on after Polonius with his naive theory of motivation is dispatched, they get no further with Hamlet than he did. When they tell the player that it 'is pointless to speak to Hamlet. Wouldn't make any difference,' Hamlet comes to the footlight and spits at the audience (which spits back). (This hostile relationship between the expectations of the motive sleuths and the failure of the author to give an easy explanation is made explicit in Stoppard's recent play *Cahoot's Macbeth* when the Czech police agent who intrudes upon a production of *Macbeth* expresses his distrust of Shakespeare. 'How do we know Shakespeare wasn't spitting at the audience, when he should have had his eye on Verona, hanging around the gents so to speak.')

When Rosencrantz and Guildenstern join their belts together to make a trap for Hamlet (who enters dragging Polonius' body) and Rosencrantz's pants 'fall slowly down,' Stoppard is not echoing the conclusion of *Waiting for Godot* through a lack of originality. The unsuccessful trap is a comment on the drama. Like Godot, Hamlet cannot be reduced to a few facts or generalizations. There is a kind of drama which does not yield to the search for motivation.

Hamlet will not reveal himself. In Act III scene ii of Shakespeare's play he challenges Guildenstern to play the recorder and then defies his attempt to play upon himself.

> HAMLET: ... give it breath with your mouth, and it will discourse most
> eloquent music.
> GUILDENSTERN: ... I have not the skill.
> HAMLET: Why, look you now, how unworthy a thing you make of me!
> You would play upon me, you would seem to know my stops, you would
> pluck out the heart of my mystery, you would sound me from my lowest
> note to the top of my compass–and there is much music, excellent voice,
> in this little organ–yet cannot you make it speak. 'Sblood, do you think
> I am easier to be played on than a pipe? Call me what instrument you will,
> though you can fret me, you cannot play upon me.

Stoppard, who also resists too easy revelation, deliberately leaves out of his play this most important scene. On the boat to England, however, the players do emerge from barrels and produce the music which Hamlet refuses to provide. And Guildenstern says, 'the pipe discourses, as the saying goes, most elequent music. A thing like that could change the course of events.' Significantly, Stoppard's play ends with music overcoming explanation. The final speech is given by Horatio (of whom Hamlet says earlier, 'thou art not a pipe.'). It is his denial that Hamlet gave command for the death of Rosencrantz and Guildenstern and his promise to tell the 'yet unknowing world' 'how these things came about,' closing with the assertion 'all this can I truly deliver.' Stoppard's final stage direction to accompany Shakespeare's dialogue reads: 'But during the above speech, the play fades out, overtaken by dark and music.'

The music that 'discourses eloquently' and 'might change the course of things' is obviously not the explanation of motive and purpose which Hamlet denies to Rosencrantz and Guildenstern and Horatio promises 'the still unknowing world' but does not get around to delivering. The music comes with the players and they act out identity not motivation.

At the first meeting with Rosencrantz and Guildenstern, heralded by 'sound of drums and flute,' the player promises 'death and disclosure, universal and particular, denouements both unexpected and inexorable.' At the end of the play Guildenstern demands, 'But why? Was it all for this? Who are we that so much should converge on our little deaths?' The player responds, 'You are Rosencrantz and Guildenstern. That's enough.' The only disclosure the players provide for Rosencrantz and Guildenstern is death. They play out the dumbshow of two murdered spies. Rosencrantz and Guildenstern recognize themselves but fail to admit what they have seen and act upon it. And the players enact a final death scene which points out the contrast between ordinary and theatrical death. Infuriated by the player's refusal to provide an explanation, Guildenstern stabs him with his own stage dagger saying, 'If we have a destiny, then so had he ... If there are no explanations for us, then let there be none for him.' The player dies convincingly and then gets up to the applause of his company. A few moments later Rosencrantz and Guildenstern simply fade into the dark

illustrating Guildenstern's point that 'Death is the absence of presence.'
'Dying is not romantic, death is not a game that will soon be over.'

If their deaths are not like those of Hamlet and the actors, that
does not mean that Rosencrantz and Guildenstern can discount what
they see enacted. Their refusal to acknowledge themselves in the
dumbshow is fatal. They hear the 'eloquent discourse' of the music
but do not act to 'change the course of things.'

Stoppard's point is clear. Although we should not look to drama
for neat answers, our very lives, like those of Rosencrantz and
Guildenstern, depend on our ability to learn from what we see on
stage. The play can teach us to see ourselves and recognize that we
are free to act even within the confines of inexorable destiny. It can
show us further the consequences of our choices. As Rosencrantz says,
'There must have been a moment when we could have said No, but
we missed it . . . next time we will know better.'

In *The Real Inspector Hound* Stoppard expanded on **Polonius'**
metaphor of the hound that hunts the trail of policy to create an anti-
play exposing the conventional expectations of audiences. Ronald
Hayman called it 'a parody of the thriller convention and the language
in which critics approach it.' But the play is more than that. It is a
comic examination of the search for ansers in **all** drama. By embodying
the conventional expectations of the audience in characters who
assume the role of police Inspector Hound in baffling succession,
Stoppard illustrates the inadequacy of old attitudes and the need
for new ones. The opening directions read:

> The first thing is that the audience appear to be confronted by their own
> reflection in a huge mirror. Impossible. However, back there in the
> gloom-not at the footlights-a bank of plush seats and pale smudges
> of faces.

Soon the image is contracted to the two critics, Birdboot and Moon,
who comment on the play in progress. Birdboot, like Polonius, ferrets
out motive that can be summed up in single word clichés: **'Revenge'**,
'Jealousy', 'the paranoid grudge'. And like Inspector Hound who has
a secret plan but has volunteers out combing the swamps with loud-
hailers, shouting, 'Don't be a madman, give yourself up,' he believes
'The answer lies out there in the swamps,' awaiting revelation. 'The
skeleton in the cupboard is coming home to roost.' He ends praising
the play for creating 'a real situation' and anticipating that it will be
resolved with a 'startling denouement.'

Moon represents a more intellectually pretentious critical
perspective, but one as ludicrous in its grandiose search for
philosophical answers as Birdboot's reductive search for psychological
answers. His clichés are those of the avant garde. For him the play is
'on the side of life', 'concerned with the notion of identity', it
asserts 'je suis . . . ergo sum' and asks the question 'Where is God? —
which Moon says gives rise to Voltaire's cry, 'Voilà!' (To the

question 'Where is God?' Birdboot responds 'Who?' and peeps furtively into his programme. 'God?') Moon also concludes with praise for the play: it has given 'in the austere framework . . . of a country house weekend a useful symbol of the human condition.'

On stage the actors play out their old-fashioned melodrama oblivious to a corpse concealed from them by stage furniture, and visible only to the audience. It is Higgs, the 'first-string' critic, the embodiment of established critical response. By the end of the play Birdboot and Moon will also become stage corpses, killed off and replaced by the 'third-string' critic Puckridge.

Birdboot, caught up in his naive identification and fascination with the actors, mounts the stage assuming the role of the philandering lady. After a few moments in this role, he is shot by an unknown and unseen assailant. He is killed just as he is about to offer the denouement he predicted earlier. He falls saying, 'I see it all.' With the demise of the critical positions represented by Higgs and Birdboot, the old roles of Hound and the melodramatic villain are no longer necessary and the actors of those roles assume the seats of the critics to comment disapprovingly on the new action as a 'ragbag,' 'not my cup of tea.'

The role of Hound, however, is like a vacuum. Moon rushes to the fallen Birdboot and is temporarily thrust into the role of Inspector Hound. 'Who did this and why?' he asks. As Hound, Moon offers explanations of the two corpses. He identifies Higgs as 'the Real McCoy' 'the Canadian who . . . meeting Gascoyne in the street and being solicited for sixpence for a toffee apple, smacked him across the ear, with the cry, "How's that for a grudge to harbor, you sniffling little workshy". Gascoyne has murdered him in revenge. In relating the encounter as given earlier by the original Inspector Hound, Moon changes the facts. In that version Gascoyne solicited sixpence for a cup of tea. The commentary on the demands of critics and audience is obvious. They bear a grudge against playwrights who expect work of them, who do not provide what they are familiar and comfortable with–'their cup of tea,' who will not serve up 'toffee apples'–sugar-coated satisfaction, and who assault them with disconcerting material.

Moon's explanation of the second corpse, Birdboot/Gascoyne, is the kind of easy denouement just discredited. 'I am now in a position to reveal the mystery,' he says, Felicity Cunningham, the ingenue, committed the murder because Gascoyne had jilted her. This explanation convinces no one and is soon abandoned. Becoming involved in the action Moon begins to examine his own motives and to accept the suggestion of Major Magnus that he has been only masquerading as police Inspector Hound and is in reality 'the stranger in our midst' responsible for the deaths of his rival critics.

Moon having reverted to his own role, the role of sleuth requires a new embodiment, Major Magnus. He strips off his disguise to reveal himself as 'the real Inspector Hound'. Moon recognizes him as Puckridge the third-string critic. It is he, Moon now realizes, who has killed off Higgs and Birdboot and now is preparing to replace Moon himself. Moon turns to run: he is too late. Puckridge shoots him.

The revelation of Puckridge-Magnus that he is not only Hound but Albert, the leading lady's lost husband, is still less convincing than the denouements suggested earlier by Birdboot and Moon. In Major Magnus the drama of revelation is reduced to its ultimate absurdity. But true to its promise, the play offers no easy summary of a new critical perspective to replace outmoded ones. Exactly what the progression from Moon to Puckridge will bring is uncertain. 'Nobody knows' what he is like as a critic we are told earlier. But it is obvious that he will offer no relief from sleuthing. Stoppard continues to confront the audience with the inadequacy of its responses and demands.

The alternative to Magnus lies in Moon. As he abandons the role of Hound to examine his own motives, he seems strangely realistic even in the midst of farcical exaggeration. If Stoppard discredits naive identification like that of Birdboot, he nevertheless asserts that drama should engage us personally and directly. It is significant in this respect that it is Moon, not Birdboot, who first responds to the telephone ringing on the empty stage.

If the play discredits the demand for easy answers in conventional forms, it does not assert that drama has no answers to provide. As Moon says, 'I think we are entitled to ask.' And he poses two questions, 'Does this play know where it's going?'; 'Does it . . . declare its affiliations?' This is, of course, a parody of critical jargon, but it is also a serious indication of what the public can expect and what can be expected of it.

The first question implies the expectation of a familiar plot. *The Real Inspector Hound* does proceed through the conventional stages of a mystery thriller from exposition through reversals to a final denouement, but only to parody the demand that this expectation be fulfilled. Within the framework of that plot it also proceeds through a recognizable presentation of critical attitudes. The play does 'know where it is going' and if not too intent on unravelling a familiar pattern of mystery, the audience can find out.

The second question implies the demand that the play be part of an established tradition. Again *The Real Inspector Hound* provides both an ironic, comic answer and a serious one. Its obvious affinities are with the tradition of Agatha Christie which it parodies. But an audience aware of a wider range of modern drama will be able to recognize it as part of the tradition of anti-plays which comment on the nature of drama itself. Chekhov's *The Cherry Orchard*, Pirandello's *Six Characters in Search of An Author*, Ionesco's *Bald Soprano*, and Brecht's *Three Penny Opera*—to name only the best known—also parody familiar structure to expose the conventional demands of the audience and illustrate their inadequacy. Not only is the audience 'entitled' to ask these questions, it must ask them if it expects to see the more significant structure and affinities of Stoppard's play.

Jumpers is also an anti-play. Again Stoppard presents a body on stage to be accounted for. The police detective, Bones; the psychiatrist, Archibald Jumper; and the servant, Crouch; succeed each other in attempts to provide a denouement. Against this plot Stoppard distends a philosophical discussion of relative versus absolute morality, which provides the terms in which murder must ultimately be accounted for.

The conventional characters of detective, psychiatrist, and servant-observer are each exposed in turn as inadequate theatrical devices. Bones appears carrying flowers and a record album by the prime suspect, Dotty, which he hopes to have autographed. He is more interested in Dotty as a theatrical personality than as a murder suspect. His attitude is, as Archie points out, 'curiously formal but somewhat dated.' The role of the sleuth is an anachronistic remnant of showbusiness. Archie in his role as psychiatrist promises to try to get Dotty 'to open up.' He examines her with his Dermatograph: 'All kinds of disturbances under the skin show up on the surface if we can learn to read it.' A modern dandy with all kinds of intellectual credentials—'doctor of medicine, philosophy, literature and law, diplomas in psychological medicine and P.T., including gym,'—the psychiatrist is nevertheless as superficial as the detective. In addition he is mechanistic, voyeuristic, pretentious, and amoral.

Crouch, the servant observer, is 'old and small and a bit stooped.' His naiveté inspires sympathy, but not initial confidence in him as a source of explanation. His 'master key' allowing him to enter the scene unannounced and unnoticed is a device as mechanistic as Archie's dermatograph. The very powers of observation which justify his function in the play are called into question in the first scene. The secretary swings back and forth on a chandelier doing a strip tease. Crouch is 'bewildered.' Every time he looks up stage the gap is empty. Finally he backs into her path and is knocked 'arse over top.' The servant-observer is faithful but creaking and no longer a trustworthy source of information.

The three conventional devices of revelation are further discredited by making them equivalent. When Bones arrives, George tells him, 'I was expecting a psychiatrist.' Later Bones assumes the role of servant bringing lunch to Dotty and Archie in order to observe them. Archie makes his first appearance by emerging from Dotty's curtained bed to see why he fails to hear the second shoe he has discarded fall. Bones has caught it in mid-air. Ironically, both Bones and Archie are more interested in exculpating Dotty than in finding the truth. The solutions they offer invert their roles. Bones, addressing Archie, offers a psychiatric explanation, 'nervous strain, appalling pressure and one day snap.' What is needed is an 'expert witness.' Archie, in conversation with Bones, provides the traditional paraphernalia of detective drama—delineation of the possible motives of the suspects, a disappearing corpse, a forged suicide note, and a coroner's certificate.

By Act III the investigations of Bones and Archie are complete and Crouch has provided his eye-witness account of the murder, but the murder is still unsolved. At this point Archie dismisses the idea that things can be accounted for, 'Life is not a mystery novel. It does not guarantee a denouement, truth for us philosophers is an interim judgement.' He departs taking Crouch with him. Immediately following Archie's declaration, Stoppard nevertheless presents two further possible denouements—one based on fact, one on metaphor. The first is the surprise introduction of a new, plausible suspect, George's secretary. Crouch has supplied the information that the murdered McFee was breaking off a secret affair with her to enter a monastery. There is at last a sufficient motive. When we see her depart in a blodstained coat, we ask if she is not the murderer. In the second denouement George discovers that he inadvertently shot his rabbit, Thumper. This discovery which could explain the blood on the secretary's coat casts a doubt on the previous denouement and prepares for the final one. Still oblivious to the physical, living world around him, George steps down backwards from his desk with a sickening crunch onto Pat, the tortoise. One foot on his desk and one on Pat, he looks down and cries, 'Help! Murder!'

This second resolution is farcical and yet we do know to believe it. The play ends by asking us to choose between the three positions about the truth revealed in drama. The first position is Archie's: that 'truth is an interim judgement'—drama can never really account for murder. The second position of that of Bones, Archie in his role of psychiatrist, and Crouch in the role of observer of past action: that truth lies in 'observable phenomena.' We account for murder by revealing previously unknown events and personal psychological values. The third position is Crouch's, but in the role of philosopher: that there are universal truths based on absolute values.

Archie is right about the play, 'we will never know who killed McFee.' Resolutions which place truth in observation, the facts of the plot, are at best arbitrary. Crouch's observation of Dotty seemed to leave little room for doubt that it was she who fired the fatal shot. But his story about McFee's plan to break off with his secretary combined with the observation of blood stains on her coat make it equally if not more plausible that the secretary did it. The discovery of Thumper leaves us wondering again. Playwrights can, of course, and usually do choose among the suspects and name the murderer, but the arbitrariness of the choice as to who will be the killer and who the red herring in *Jumpers* is too evidently merely theatrical manipulation to be accepted. That interpretation reduces the play to the show business of Bones or the voyeuristic but unproductive psychological probing of Archie.

The second resolution (the one with which Stoppard ends) is the one we must accept. If no one saw who fired the shot that killed McFee, we do know that George fired the arrow on which Thumper is impaled and that Pat is crunched under his foot because George has no awareness of him. Murder is explained by the absence from the real world of the moral absolutes which George espouses in the abstract. Dottie's cries of 'Murder, Rape, Wolves' were not as George calls them 'gratuitous acts of lupine delinquency' disturbing the more important work of a philosopher. They were true descriptions of real situations requiring a response. In his indifference, George is the guilty party. George's culpability for his inaction was suggested earlier in the play in an allusion to the scene in *Hamlet* where Hamlet observes Claudius at prayers and contemplates his murder. Bones arrives:

> [*George*] *(marches to the door, brandishing his bow and arrow and putting his mouth to the tortoise ear, or thereabouts, confides in it.)* Now I might do it, Pat.

Although it is Stoppard and not Crouch who offers this final explanation of murder, it is nevertheless a view of events associated with Crouch's attitude. He alone among those whose role in the play is to provide explanation sees and articulates the crisis brought about by the practical absence of absolutes in daily life. And he is the one character able to unite moral absolutes with practical application. It is Crouch who reports the murder. He who knows exactly when the absence of absolute moral values becomes crucial to McFee–'It was the astronauts fighting on the moon that finally turned him.' And he is able to respond with human concern while still asserting moral absolutes. 'Don't worry your head about it,' he tells McFee, 'that astronaut jobbo is good for twenty years hard.' His response to McFee is in direct contrast with those of George and Archie to Dotty's expression of distress at the same crisis:

> ... Man is on the Moon, his feet on solid ground, and he has seen us whole, all in one go, *little–local* ... and all our absolutes, the thou-shalts and the thou-shalt-nots that seemed to be the very condition of our existence, how did they look to two moonmen with a single neck to save between them? Like the local customs of another place. When that thought drips through to the bottom, people won't just carry on.

Having just heard the answer, Archie can still do no more than repeat his clichéd psychiatric question, 'When did you first become aware of these feelings?' Dotty in tears ignores him and cries out, 'Georgie,' but George 'can't or won't' respond and retreats into a philosophical anecdote about Wittgenstein. (Ironically, not one affirming the absolutes he espouses but one illustrating the relativity of our perceptions.)

In the coda, Crouch sits as Chairman of the inquiry into 'Man: Good, Bad, or Indifferent.' His two interventions confirm that it is the role of philosophy in drama to seek answers: When the archbishop refers to his sins, Crouch asks, 'What does he mean by that?' His second intervention comes as the jumpers begin threatening the archbishop. George cries 'Point of Order.' The archbishop pleads 'Help me, George.' Crouch offers George a chance to become involved in the inquiry, 'Do you have any questions for this witness, professor?' George again refuses to engage his philosophy practically, explaining '... this seems to be a political ground ... Surely only a proper respect for absolute values ... universal truths–philosophy ... ' He is interrupted by the shot which knocks the archbishop from the pyramid and kills him. Again George's contribution to murder is evident.

If Crouch were only an impersonal observer–a device to establish facts and motives–he would be just another theatrical cliché ultimately as expendable to drama as Bones or Archie, but Crouch is more than an observer. He provides a serious philosophical perspective that Bones and Archie do not. They are detective and psychiatrist but their 'real interests,' as they confess, are show business and the trampoline. Crouch's interest is philosophy. Underlying his actions is a system of serious beliefs and values. He operates from the moral conviction which is the mainspring of the greatest drama: that there is right and wrong and that those who do not act accordingly are guilty and will answer for their actions. He may be dispensable as a servant observer but in his new role as arbiter of philosophy– the director of the inquiry–drama must make a place for him.

In *Artist Descending a Staircase* and *After Magritte*, Stoppard continues his attack upon rationalized explanation of apparently contradictory accounts of observed phenomena. Seen in the context of his other works, these plays can be recognized as part of Stoppard's successful comic illustration of the triviality of the questions and answers provided by much conventional theatre. In the radio play *Artist Descending* the sounds of a tape which seems to be an accurate recording of the events of a murder or suicide are reproduced exactly by the banal action of swatting a fly. In *After Magritte* the characters describe what they think they saw on the street outside. One thinks it was a uniformed football

Mother (Judy Wilson), Det. Insp. Foot (C.J. Allen), Reginald Harris (Tim Thomas), Thelma Harris (Cherith Mellor) in a Young Vic production of *After Magritte*.   (Photograph by Christopher Pearce)

player with shaving cream on his face, carrying a walking stick, a ball under his arm while playing hopscotch; another thinks it was a white-bearded, one-legged blind man carrying a large toitoise (or perhaps a Christmas pudding) and his white cane; another thinks it might have been a street musician with a gourd or perhaps it was a doyen from the Victoria Palace Happy Minstrel Troupe in costume. At the end of the play all the apparent mystery has been elucidated: The man was police inspector Foot himself who had interrupted his shaving to rush out to feed the parking meter in one leg of his hastily donned pyjamas carrying his wife's handbag and umbrella. There is a cry of 'lights,' a hanging lamp descends. The inspector turns to the constable who has been investigating a set of equally suspicious phenomena inside the house and says, 'I think you owe us all an explanation.'

Together, these plays constitute a noteworthy accomplishment. No playwright in English has contributed so much to the twentieth century tradition of self-commentary in drama. And unlike most of his predecessors, Stoppard has not been content to concentrate on the inadequacy of the old questions and answers. He has expanded the dialogue by also affirming what drama *can* do. He has identified what may be salvaged from the past tradition and pointed out new directions.

Stoppards contribution in *Rosencrantz and Guildenstern* alone is likely to win him a permanent place in English literature. There he has offered, if only indirectly, a careful, perceptive reading of *Hamlet* which raises questions inherent in the text. It is a reading which counterbalances the opposing tendency of the age toward psychological explanation exemplified in Earnest Jones' Freudian interpretation. By providing this reading in the form of drama itself Stoppard has produced a critical touchstone in a mode particularly characteristic of this century. As a representative view of Shakespeare *Rosencrantz and Guildenstern Are Dead* seems likely to be read along with Thomas Rhymer on *Othello,* Dryden's *All for Love,* and 'Essay of Dramatic Poesy'. Dr. Johnson's 'Preface to Shakespeare', Coleridge's essays on *Hamlet,* De Quincy's 'On the Knocking at the Gate in *Macbeth*', and A.C. Bradley's character analyses in *Shakesperian Tragedy.*

Stoppard's achievement extends beyond his contribution to the twentieth century commentary on drama. Having asserted the playwright's freedom from the fixation on the drama of motivation and plot which moves relentlessly toward tidy denouement, he has gone on to write plays free of these constraints. Once the audience gives up the role of Inspector Hound and comes to see Stoppard as a propositional playwright, it can more easily see the new structures which have replaced the old ones.

Every Good Boy Deserves Favour, is explicitly propositional. It moves toward illustration rather than toward theatrical explanation. The proposition it examines is stated directly as a geometrical postulate: 'a triangle is the shortest distance between three points' i.e., the exploitation of concern for loved ones is the state's most effective means of coercion. Its structure is the crescendo of growing emotional tension created by the triangular conflict between a coercive police state, a prisoner of conscience, and his young son. The metaphor of the triangle both as a geometric form and a musical instrument is evident in the division of the stage into three lighted areas: the prisoner's cell, the prison psychiatrist's office and the boy's school room with an orchestra in the middle. It points to the play as the illustration of a theorem and to its musical structure.

The almost negligible plot is an ironic anachronism also elucidating the proposition examined in the play. Its resolution depends upon comic inversion of one of the most hackneyed devices of theatre. The dissident Alexander Ivanov is freed from psychiatric prison because a case of mistaken identity arises, not because it is cleared up. He is mistaken by the colonel for his cellmate because their names are the same. Asked the wrong questions, he gives the satisfactory answers which he refused out of conscience to give earlier. This inversion of conventional plot suggests the identity of the man considered insane because he hears an orchestra in his head and the man committed by the state because he hears the inner voice of conscience. The arbitrary absurdity of the resolution points out that the brutal triangle is an abiding moral problem which cannot be eliminated by quick and easy means.

In his television play *Professional Foul* Stoppard again juxtaposes a comic version of traditional plot and motivation and explicit philosophical propositions. He presents us with the familiar conflict of conscience and intrigue of a TV spy drama. The play creates suspense by asking whether an American professor of moral philosophy attending a conference in Prague will overcome his original scruples and smuggle the manuscript of his former student, now a dissident, out of Czechoslovakia. It ends with a surprise when he uses unexpected means to get the manuscript through customs. One blatantly motivated 'reversal of principle' allows the professor to counteract the authority of his host government by deciding to smuggle the manuscript. A second reversal, this time totally unexplained, allows him to sneak the manuscript past officials in the luggage of another unsuspecting philosopher circumventing his right of moral choice.

The real question raised by the play, however, is not whether a manuscript will leave Czechoslovakia, but whether morality derives from the individual's sometimes inarticulate, intuitive sense of right and wrong or from the collective values of the State codified in language.

The climax illustrates the proposition that the State, like individuals, can breach the principles of free speech. Despite the expression of its values in high-sounding laws and constitutions, the State has no right to suppress individual expression, which is the ultimate source of values, on the grounds of preserving public welfare. The Czech official who silences Professor MacKendrick's lecture on individual and public morality by deceitfully announcing that there is a fire backstage is wrong. In the words of an American Justice, 'The right to free speech does not include the right to shout fire in a crowded auditorium.'

Many of the difficulties which have beset the reception of Stoppard's plays based less explicitly on philosophical propositions become less troublesome when the propositional structure of those plays is also recognized. The audience may have other reservations about *Night and Day*, (which is not Stoppard at his best) but it no longer needs to complain as Robert Brustein has that the heroine, Ruth, is not Desdemona or Hedda Gabler. It can at least come to accept Ruth not as a realistic study but as an embodiment of the reading public which recognizes the worth of the idealism of the young journalist Jacob. It can see that the plot of her growing attraction for him and loss when he is killed moves not toward an explanation of her character and events or resolution of her romantic dilemma. Like *Every Good Boy* and *Professional Foul*, the play moves toward the illustration of a proposition. After presenting the tawdry faults of modern journalism and cataloguing the threats to a free press, it asserts at its climax that a free press, with all the superficiality and sensationalism that complete freedom entails, is worth dying for. Ruth thumbs through the pages of a London paper and asks 'What page is it on . . . That thing worth dying for?' She goes on:

> As far as I'm concerned, Jake died for the product. He died for the women's page, and the crossword, and the racing results, and the heartbreak beauty queens and somewhere at the end of a long list I suppose he died for the leading article too, but it's never worth that–

Guthrie, the cynical reporter, replies

> People do awful things to each other. But it's worse in places where

Tristan Tzara (John Hurt), Gwendolen (Maria Aitken), James Joyce (Tom Bell) in *Travesties* by the RSC at the Aldwych 1974.   (Photograph by Sophie Baker)

everybody is kept in the dark. It really is. Information is light. Information, in itself, about anything, is light. That's all you can say, really.

If we already know this, we nevertheless need to be reminded of it and to assimilate it intellectually and emotionally. By making this realization rather than a more expected psychological one the culmination of *Night and Day*, Stoppard focuses attention on permanent ideas rather than another examination of romantic motivations.

The objection that *Travesties* lacks form and purpose (typified by Tynan's response) also stems from the failure to recognize its propositional structure and complex use of plot. Ostensibly, the play is a travesty of Wilde, using the plot of *The Importance of Being Earnest* with James Joyce, the dadaist Tristan Tzara and a British consular official Henry Carr in the major roles. But as the plural title suggests, there is also a second more fundamental parallel with Joyce's *Ulysses*. Like Joyce's novel, Stoppard's play manipulates a parallel between a pre-existing literary plot–*The Importance of Being Earnest*–and events drawn partly from life and partly from imagination–the appearance in Zurich during World War I of Joyce, Tzara, Lenin and the two minor British Consular officials, Bennett and Carr. And like *Ulysses*, *Travesties* employs a variety of contrasting styles in episodic succession to reflect the events enacted or to serve as indirect commentary on them. Joyce, the serious artist, catechizes Tzara, the dadaist, in the style of the 'Ithaca' episode of *Ulysses*; Tzara, the Roumanian clown, greets Joyce, the irreverent Irishman, in a scene composed entirely of limericks, etc.

As Stoppard points out in the play, the choice of Homer's *Odyssey* for his plot was in itself a conscious statement by Joyce about the nature of heroism. Stoppard's choice of Wilde's play is also a statement. In contrast to the *Odyssey*, there is no importance to Wilde's plot; it is only a vehicle for observations and commentary which are the serious purpose of the play. That is, of course, the case with *Travesties*.

The serious commentary of *Travesties* is the examination of the three revolutionaries–Joyce, Lenin and Tzara–who converge in Zurich during World War I. By juxtaposing the three, the play argues the propositions that art is more revolutionary than politics and that the apolitical and socially conservative Joyce is more revolutionary than Tzara the anti-social, flamboyantly radical dadaist. Tzara uses tradition destructively cutting up Shakespeare's Sonnett XVIII into scraps, shaking them in a hat, and drawing them out randomly to produce a new dadaist poem. Joyce uses tradition constructively. Out of the same hat used by Tzara, Joyce pulls first a flower–a white carnation which he bestows on Tzara who affixes it to his lapel in Wildean exhibitionism. Then in a greater feat of magic he pulls out a rabbit which is equated with his creation of Leopold Bloom– the common man as a complete and human hero. This act surpasses both Tzara and Lenin. *Ulysses* is a greater artistic achievement than anything produced by the dadaists and it does more than Lenin's political revolution to give dignity to the common man.

In the end, however, there is still place for Tzara's Wildean posturing and irreverance. The play ends with a scene in the style of a music hall song reminiscent of the dadaists' antics at their Zurich headquarters in the Cabaret Voltaire. While there is a place for what Tzara and Wilde represent, it is obviously secondary. *Travesties* is full of clever Wildean epigrams, but the method of its major commentary is that of *Ulysses*. The changing styles of presentation reveal an evaluation of the three revolutionaries. Once we acknowledge that fact, the section on Lenin interpolated in Wilde's plot which has so troubled the critics can be recognized not as an ungainly impediment but as an integral part of an identifiable structure. Like Molly's retrospective appraisal of Bloom in the 'Penelope' episode of *Ulysses*, the appraisal of Lenin is presented through the memories of his wife. The amalgam of Lenin's own speeches, letters, official pronouncements and literary judgements which she remembers define the man. He is discursive, prosaic, didactic, and artistically reactionary. As in all Stoppard's works there are serious concerns and an integral structure behind the comic facade of *Travesties*. Their recognition, however, depends upon a more careful scrutiny than the play has received.

Stoppard's significant achievement in calling the attention of his audience to its conventional assumptions about the function of drama and in writing plays which provide a different kind of question and answer is there for those willing to look closely enough to see it. Critics who still withhold acknowledgement of Stoppard's accomplishment because they have substituted facile metaphors for the more careful and extensive examination his plays require, and because they cling to conventional expectations, are wrong. It is time for them to be less workshy, to abandon the role of Inspector Hound, give up demands for toffee apples and their cup of tea. When that is done, Stoppard can be removed from the critical limbo to which he has been unjustly relegated. He can be recognized for what he is: a serious and important playwright who has made a lasting contribution to modern drama.

NIGHT AND DAY
Judy Simons

Tom Stoppard's *Night and Day* enjoyed a lengthy run at the Phoenix
theatre in London's West End, and a similar success is predicted for
Broadway. It played to packed houses and attracted three famous
actresses to its central role. But how major a contribution to English drama
is this piece of inspired theatrical dialectic about British journalism? And
how impressive an artistic figure is its author? Is he a serious artist, whose
works will loom large in examination syllabuses of the future, or is he
merely, as has been asserted,

> beloved by those for whom the theatre is an end and not a means, diversionary
> and not central, a ramification and not a modifier of the status quo, a
> soother of worried minds and not an irritant.[1]

The question of the relationship of popular commercial success to enduring
artistic merit is a problematic one. Does the presence of the former
necessarily invalidate the latter? The image of the best seller has become
tarnished since Dickens' day and is not always one with which the
committed contemporary artist wishes to be associated. Even Stoppard
himself has difficulty in reconciling the two areas of his reputation. In
discussing his plays, he has endorsed the opinion that,

> it is a matter of taste whether one says they're wonderfully frivolous
> saddened by occasional seriousness, or whether there's a serious play,
> irredeemably ruined by the frivolous side of the man's nature.[2]

It is significant that in his survey of recent British theatre, Kerensky
excludes Stoppard from the section on politically committed dramatists,
and admits him instead, rather uncomfortably, to the chapter entitled
'Domestic Bliss', dealing with popular dramatists who analyse marriage, a
subject with which Stoppard has displayed no clearly identifiable concern.

His notorious difficulty of categorization is an indication of his
originality, but his acknowledged technical dazzle should not be a deceptive
factor in his assessment, for as his work has progressed, his major plays do
reveal a development of certain central pertinent themes with which he has
become increasingly involved.

Travesties' deliberate questioning of the role of the artist in society
can be read as a statement of self-awareness, a form of self-questioning
on Stoppard's part, and it is a question answered with growing authority
by the forms and content of his later plays. Lenin's speech in that play

concerning art and censorship suggests the need for artistic appraisal and self justification. While obviously critical of Lenin's attitude, Stoppard implicitly queries the moral ambiguity of the artist's position.

> LENIN: . . . We want to establish and we shall establish a free press, free not simply from the police, but also from capital, from careerism, and what is more, free from bourgeois individualism! . . . we must say to you bourgeois individualists that your talk about absolute freedom is sheer hypocrisy. There can be no real and effective freedom in a society based on the power of money. Are you free in relation to your bourgeois publisher, Mr. Writer? And in relation to your bourgeois public which demands that you provide it with pornography? The freedom of the bourgeois writer, artist or actor is simply disguised dependence on the money-bag, on corruption, on prostitution.[3]

The irony at the heart of the speech, while comic in intention and effect for the abuse of logic employed, does display a basic unease at the relationship between the artist and the social structure within which he works, an area of personal concern for the dramatist. Discussing the comic characteristics of his plays, Stoppard has acknowledged his debt to Beckett and the manifestation of the absurd in his own work.

> There's a Beckett joke which is the funniest joke in the world to me. It appears in various forms, but it consists of confident statement followed by immediate refutation in the same voice. It's a constant process of elaborate structure and sudden–and total–dismantlement.[4]

Lenin's speech, one example of this technique which is central to all the plays, anticipates the arguments presented by President Mageeba in *Night and Day*, a play which provides a specific framework, through its central subject of journalism, for exploring the nature of literary freedom and artistic responsibility.

> MAGEEBA: . . . At the time of independence the Daily Citizen was undoubtedly free. It was free to select the news it thought fit to print, to make much of it or little, and free to make room for more and more girls wearing less and less underwear. You may smile, but does freedom of the press mean freedom to choose its own standards?[5]

The similarities between Mageeba's speech and Lenin's, the two exponents of diametrically opposed political stances, establish the irony central to Stoppard's vision of ideology as myth. And these speeches are by no means isolated instances of a tone of serious enquiry in Stoppard's oeuvre. The possibilities regarding absolutes, freedom, choice, morality and ethics have been preoccupations reflected in Stoppard's earlier work. His first major popular success, *Rosencrantz and Guildenstern Are Dead* established his concern with themes of chance, time, and the nature of individual identity, and these philosophical concerns are developed within the more precise contexts of his later plays to acquire a directly political relevance. The characteristic verbal and structural ambiguities of his writing have definite thematic significance in reflecting the problematic quality

John Thaw, William Marlow and Olu Jacobs in *Night and Day* at the Phoenix
Theatre.   (Photograph by John Haynes)

of communication, the arbitrariness of individual choice, and the un-
certainties of social ethics. The development in his work has been through
the growing commitment and confidence evident in the confined settings
and positive arguments presented with a precision and a clarity lacking
in his earlier writings.

His three most recent plays, *Every Good Boy Deserves Favour,
Professional Foul* and *Night and Day* have all confronted quite directly
the subject of individual freedom. *Every Good Boy Deserves Favour*
and *Professional Foul*, both set in countries behind the Iron Curtain,
present the restrictions on freedom of speech and consequently on
action within a totalitarian state, and articulate ethical and philosophical
aspects of conflict between the state and the individual. The background
of violence in the relaistic environment allowed by the medium of
television in *Professional Foul* is theatrically realised through the use of
the orchestra in *Every Good Boy Deserves Favour*, establishing the
metaphor of the dissident as 'the discordant note, one might say, in an
orchestrated society'[6] and evolving a series of dramatic contrasts;
between noise and silence, fiction and fact, sanity and madness. The
environment of the Soviet mental hospital becomes an effective image
of the State, while presenting both a naturalistic demonstration of
constraint and its psychological effects, plus a poetic image of enclosure.

The two plays also suggest an extension of the central theme of the
repression of a totalitarian regime by considering the effects of such

a situation on the conscience of Western liberal democracy. Anderson, the professor of ethics in *Professional Foul*, is forced into direct confrontation between ethical theory and political fact, and his response indicates the level of commitment, courage and concern necessary to be even slightly effective. His speech to the colloquium and his smuggling the dissident thesis display a reversal of his original principles when faced with the harsh realities of a repressive system:

> There is a sense of right and wrong which precedes utterance. It is individually experienced and it concerns one person's dealings with another. From this experience we have built a system of ethics which is the sum of individual acts of recognition of individual right. If this is so, the implications are serious for a collective or State ethic which finds itself in conflict with individual rights, and seeks in the name of the people, to impose its value on the very individuals who comprise the state. [7]

The analysis of the complexity of ethical issues extends our perception of the situation and gives depth to the superficial simplicity of the emotive cause of the persecuted writer in a repressive regime. Anderson himself must work against the individual ethic by use of McKendrick who unwittingly smuggles the thesis through customs. This denial of a basic individual right, the abuse of McKendrick's individual freedom is justified in the terms of the play, partly by the presentation of McKendrick as a loudmouthed boor, but also by the very nature of the issues involved. The seriousness of purpose and directness of tone of the speech introduce a new element into this later work of Stoppard's, at variance with the intellectual and verbal gymnastics of his earlier plays which, as he admitted, in order to succeed 'must be entirely untouched by any suspicion of usefulness.'[8]

The dedication of *Every Good Boy Deserves Favour* to Victor Fainberg and Vladimir Bukovsky, the two Russian dissidents, together with Stoppard's long introductory note on the play, reinforce this element of commitment and his new approach to the role of artisitic responsibility, previously only tentatively explored:

> Exceptional courage is a quality drawn from certain people in exceptional conditions. Although British society is not free of abuse, we are not used to meeting courage because conditions do not demand it (I am not thinking of the courage with which people face, say, an illness or a bereavement).[9]

The dramatization of these conditions for courage continues in a more subtle arena in the naturalistic setting of *Night and Day*, in the black African state of Kambawe. It is a play which establishes a complex dialectic structure, and in these terms is a natural extension of the work that has preceded it. Parallels between the black African dictatorship and western (British) democracy are drawn so that the two, apparent political antitheses, become analogous in their capacity for allowing genuine freedom of speech and action, and comparable also with conditions in a communist state.

The major theme is presented through discussion of the freedom of the press and the play is constructed around a central irony. Richard Wagner, an experienced Fleet Street journalist on a prestigious Sunday newspaper, *The Sunday Globe*, arrives in Kambawe to cover a story of a possible political coup, only to find that a scoop for his paper has been written by a naive, provincial, freelance reporter, who came by the story accidentally. Discovering that the young reporter resigned his post on *The Grimsby Evening Messenger*, having made an individual stand against an NUJ strike, Wagner, a union activist, manoeuvres his colleagues in London so that *The Sunday Globe* closes in protest–on the day that Wagner himself has a scoop to be published. The formal plot makes Stoppard's moral structurally explicit with ironic simplicity when Wagner finds himself the victim of the union consolidation he had sought as protection through personal rather than ideological motives, and it implicitly questions the ethical basis of ideology.

It has been said that Stoppard's early plays 'reel away from seriousness as from a contagious disease'[10] but this later work, while maintaining the comic tone, does confront the implications of ideology for the individual fully and directly. The indictment of socialist concepts of union militancy and the closed shop parallels the attack on repressive totalitarianism in earlier work and does not ignore criticism of capitalist exploitation. The analysis of varying political structures is untouched by romanticism in the approach to individualism, and avoids the sentimentalism apparent in the Hollar episode of *Professional Foul*, where a child is made an innocent and halting interpreter of his parents' predicament. Unlike obvious 'political' dramatists of the 'fifties and 'sixties, such as Osborne or Wesker, often naive in their glamorization of the individual's struggle against social evils, Stoppard's scepticism extends to his portrayal of the egoism which he sees as dominating professional, political and social relations.

In exploring aspects of the nature of press freedom, Stoppard considers the function of the press and the abuse of the medium by journalists. His stylistic versatility is used to mock Grub Street techniques in the facile adaptation of individual style to suit the particular 'hat' worn by any newspaper. Describing the interpretations of the political events in Kambawe, Wagner reads from a range of press reports.

> WAGNER: 'The smouldering heart of this coffee-laden, copper loaded corner of Africa is being ripped apart by the ambitions of a cashiered Colonel whose iron fist, UN observers fear, may turn out to be holding a hammer and sickle' . . . *(He tosses that aside and reads from the front page of the New York Times.)* 'Jeddu, Saturday. This time last week Jeddu was a one-horse town on the road from Kamba City to nowhere. Today you can't see the town for cavalry, mainly armoured personnel carriers and a few T-47 tanks. In them thar hills to the north-west, the renegade Colonel Shimbu is given no more chance than Colonel Custer– if only he'd stand still. Unfortunately, no one can find the Colonel to tell him to stop playing the Indians and it may be that Jeddu is

going to wake up one morning with its armoured cars drawn up in a circle.' *(He throws that aside.)* I hate them and their Pulitzer Prizes. All writing and no facts. *(The Sunday Times.)* 'At five minutes past eight on Wednesday morning, an aide-de-camp on the staff of Supreme Commander and President Ginku Mageeba, his uniform distinguished by Christian Dior sunglasses and unbuttoned flies, drove a green and white jeep up to the Princess Alice Bar in downtown Jeddu and commandeered it as the nerve centre of Mageeba's victorious drive against the forces of darkness, otherwise known as the Adoma Liberation Front. The army itself appeared in time for elevenses, and by today the advance had nearly reached the Esso pump three hundred yards up the road towards the enemy.' Very funny. All facts and no news. *(He looks briefly through the Mirror.)* Nothing. Well, that's honest anyway.[11]

It is evident that the reports are not only contradictory, but are akin to fiction in their flagrant distortion of actuality. Wagner's acceptance of the distinction between 'facts' and 'news' is a tacit admission of the journalist's role as anything but a communicator of truth, and Ruth Carson emphasises this point, talking about her small son's literary ambitions: 'I'll buy him a reporter doll for Christmas. Wind it up and it gets it wrong.'[12] The facility for capturing cliches employed by journalists and parodied here is more than an exhibition of verbal ingenuity; it exposes pretensions both to literary quality and literary freedom. Stoppard, himself an ex-journalist, does not flinch from criticism of the complacency and effrontery of those who consider that writing, however misused, because a tool of art

Diana Rigg and Peter Machin in *Night and Day* at the Phoenix Theatre.
(Photograph by John Haynes)

and a potential expression of individual freedom, is consequently more worthwhile professionally than the manual skill involved in printing and typesetting.

> MILNE: We were called out for the same reason as the Mirror last year—because the printers had got a new deal.
> WAGNER: *(High)* Well, there were printers getting more than journalists!
> MILNE: Yes, I know, but you make it sound as if the natural order has been overthrown. Fish sing in the streets, rivers run uphill, and the printers are getting more than the journalists. Okay—you're worth more than a printer. But look at some of this—
> *(With his hand, or perhaps his foot,* MILNE *spreads the newspapers and the* News of the World *lies in front of him.)* 'Exposed! The Ouija Board Widow Who's Writing Hitler's Memoirs' . . . 'It was Frying Tonight and Every Night In the Back Of The Chip Shop . . . .' 'Some Like It Hot And Sweet—Sally Smith was a tea lady in a Blackpool engineering works, but it was the way she filled those C-cups which got our cameraman all stirred up!' It's crap. And it's written by grown men earning maybe ten thousand a year. If I was a printer, I'd look at some of the stuff I'm given to print, and I'd ask myself what is supposed to be so special about the people who write it.[13]

The parody has a purpose beyond the overt satire when the attack continues unsparingly on the abuse of the medium and the misconceptions of public opinion.

> MILNE: People think that rubbish journalism is produced by men of discrimination who are vaguely ashamed of truckling to the lowest taste. But it's not. It's produced by people doing their best work. Proud of their expertise with a limited number of cheap devices to put a shine on the shit.[14]

The dramatic conflict between Wagner and Milne central to the play's structure, becomes more than a conflict between experience and naivety. It forms a comment on and an exposure of experience, through Wagner's subordination of personal values and the demands of professional pride, and his clear abuse of friendship and trust. His evident preference for the telex machine over the womanly attractions presented by Ruth is symptomatic of his total emotional aridity. It is an integral irony of his portrayal that his characterization is in itself a cliché: he is the typical caricature of a hard-bitten Australian pressman. The cliché on which journalists depend for their livelihood become a part of them: more than just words, they become inescapably ingrained into the personality. Jacob Milne, himself a stereotype of youthful high-mindedness, does not escape what Stoppard cynically presents as the inevitable fate of romantic heroism. Simultaneously, the play is an exposure of cynical experience and naive idealism. The death of Milne realises the futility of high personal standards in a world controlled by expediency and communication designed for and produced by the mass:

> RUTH: . . . I'm not going to let you think he died for free speech and the guttering candle of democracy—crap! You're all doing it to impress each other and be top dog the next time you're propping up a bar in Beirut or Bangkok or Chancery Lane. . . . It's all bloody ego. And the winner isn't democracy, it's just business. As far as I'm concerned, Jake died for the product. He died for the women's page and the crossword and the racing

83

> results and the heartbreak beauty queens and somewhere at the end of a
> long list I suppose he died for the leading article too, but it's never worth
> that . . . [15]

Ruth's bitterness establishes her commentary as the heart of the play. Even
Guthrie's defence of the commercial position that 'Information is light.
Information in itself about anything is light'[16] while momentarily
convincing becomes overshadowed by the cynicism of the play's ethical
attitude. Both political and moral idealism are seen as subordinated to
egoism, whether it be Milne or Wagner who is the victim. The subject of
journalism is here used merely as a focus for the exploration of the issues
raised in the earlier plays. As early as 1974, Stoppard anticipated the
evolution of *Night and Day* and accurately predicted the critical response
it might receive:

> I'd like to write a play—say XYZ—which would pertain to anything from a
> Latin American coup to the British Left, and when I've done it, I'll still
> be asked why I don't write political plays.[17]

Night and Day is as directly political in its implications as are *Every Good
Boy Deserves Favour* and *Professional Foul* and can be seen as a
continuation of the arguments of *Jumpers* and *Travesties*, both of which
investigated relationships between politics, morality and art.

The question of political and professional freedom presented in *Night
and Day* is balanced too with the question of freedom on the level of
individual relationships, through the focus on Ruth Carson, the only
woman character, seen through (and seeing through) her roles of sexual
being and social animal. The technique of making the audience privy
to Ruth's thoughts, by giving her a spoken commentary inaudible to
other characters on stage, reinforces the concept of the 'split' personality,
the identity invisible to others, concealed by the masks of behaviour as
skilfully as the journalist changes his metaphoric 'hat'.

Stoppard's departure from the unconventional theatrical structure
previously dominating his work to the constraints of the 'well made play'
is in itself a demonstration of the imposition of an external force on
individual freedom of choice. *Night and Day* and *Professional Foul* both
exhibit a progressive plot, a naturalistic situation and solid realistic
characterization. Hayman's criticism of *Professional Foul* is typical:

> Since his work for stage and radio is so distinctive, it is disappointing to
> find that when he writes for television, he is content with a script much
> of which could have been produced by any competent screenwriter.[18]

This sense of disappointment at the lack of overt experimentation is
continued in some critical response to *Night and Day*, a view difficult
to reconcile with the earlier charge of self conscious virtuosity:

> Mr. Stoppard has written a deeply disappointing play . . . The crux of the
> play, to start with, is suspiciously ambiguous for so subtle an artist . . .
> Nor is there comfort to be found in the play's debate, wide, but not deep;

it suggests that Mr. Stoppard—an even more astonishing thought—has put his view-point before his drama, and thus sacrificed the effect of both.[19]

What seems to have been ignored here is the direct thematic relevance of Stoppard's deliberate choice of a conventional framework, when seen in the context of his arguments about social and artistic responsibility. Talking about his working methods to Ronald Hayman, Stoppard acknowledged the restrictions he invariably realised:

> HAYMAN: Could there be some unconscious pressure that persuades you to make promises that will limit your freedom and cut off the space of time in which you're at liberty to write anything you like?
> STOPPARD: Yes, I suppose there is, but it's really more a matter of mad optimism. I never construct these traps for myself. I work out how long I'll need to do the thing I'm doing and I'm liable to say 'Well, I'll be free in six months and I'd be quite interested to do this.' And I find in six months everything has gone wrong and I'm not free at all and I'll be free six months after that.[20]

The emphasis here on the vocabulary of liberty, choice and restriction illustrates Stoppard's personal awareness of the pressures of practical existence in any structured society. All social and professional restraints challenge the nature of individual choice and have significance in the debate on the scope and potential of human behaviour and endeavour.

Commenting on the writing of *Jumpers*, Stoppard said how much he enjoyed 'the rules that philosophers play by. It's an extremely formal discipline'[21] and this is reflected by his selection of an artistic discipline in *Night and Day*. The clear cut outline and the use of traditional dramatic devices does not, however, inhibit the levels of articulation of the play.

In his review of the first night, Irving Wardle recognised the achievement:

> Stoppard has always excelled in inventing theatrical forms for whatever he wants to talk about; but even for him it is a signal triumph to have related to such remote subjects within the discipline of a nuts and bolts naturalistic play.[22]

The arguments about press freedom invite the questioning of aspects of social, political and personal freedom, and establish a series of comparisons between professional demands and political manipulation. The complex thematic interweaving achieved in the play ironically demonstrates the freedom possible for the individual within an imposed and organised framework. The linguistic and comic brilliance which are Stoppard's acknowledged trademarks, are directed purposefully, and help to illustrate rather than conceal the serious social and political analysis at the heart of Stoppard's writing.

Notes

1.   Philip Roberts. 'Tom Stoppard: Serious Artist or Siren', *Critical Quarterly*, Autumn 1978, pp 84-91.

2. Interview with Steve Grant in *Time Out*. Quoted Kerensky, *The New British Drama,* 1977, p.155.
3. Tom Stoppard, *Travesties,* Act III.
4. Interview with R. Hayman, *Tom Stoppard*, 1978, p. 7.
5. Tom Stoppard, *Night and Day,* Act II.
6. Tom Stoppard,introduction to *Every Good Boy Deserves Favour,* 1977.
7. Tom Stoppard, *Professional Foul.*
8. Interview with Ronal Hayman, *Tom Stoppard,* 1977.
9. Tom Stoppard, introduction to *Every Good Boy Deserves Favour.*
10. Roberts, ibid.
11. Tom Stoppard, *Night and Day,* Act I.
12. ibid.
13. ibid.
14. ibid.
15. Tom Stoppard, *Night and Day,* Act II.
16. ibid.
17. Tom Stoppard, 'Ambushes for the Audience. Towards a High Comedy of Ideas', *Theatre Quarterly,* 1974.
18. Ronald Hayman, ibid. p. 137.
19. Bernard Levin, *The Sunday Times,* 12th November, 1978.
20. Hayman, ibid. p. 141.
21. Hayman, ibid. p. 1.
22. Irving Wardle, *The Times,* Nov 10, 1978.

REVIEWS OF PLAYS

TOM FOOL by Franz Xaver Kroetz (trans. Estella Schmid & Maurice Colbourne)

(Half Moon; June 1980)

For those who might find it disconcerting to be presented, live on stage, with episodes from life, I cannot recommend *Tom Fool*. Not to have experienced it, however, must have been like walking down a side street listening to a transistor radio while the parade passed by. Let me explain.

Kroetz, better known east of Berlin than west, has a marked preference for the visual. He is cautious with dialogue, and thereby heightens the importance of the few words he considers suitable. As a prelude to the breakdown of a working-class family he includes a scene of relentless boredom and unremitting tension—the son Ludwig (Michael Packer) gets out of bed, dresses, washes, brushes teeth, preens. Mother (Rachel Bell as Martha) tidies the kitchen, makes coffee, puts away the bedlinen, re-arranges the bed-settee. Simply, demonstratively, Kroetz establishes the relationship and the problems: in the space of three hours there are no compromises and no solutions both in terms of material and style.

Everything characterizes the boredom of work: an apartment is furnished to type (designer Mick Bearwish)—giant TV, flowered carpets, fake veneer. Otto, the father (Robert Hamilton), only finds escape in fantasizing as a test pilot with balsa-wood gliders; Martha reiterates proverbs and clichés in programmed response to every eventuality; Ludwig is uninspired and resorts to stealing from his mother to pay for a rock concert. The only distinguishable motivation in their mutual existence is money: it can bring harmony (the family goes to a Bierkeller); it can bring discord (the father constantly nags Ludwig to find *work*); it can interrupt lovemaking (Otto is preoccupied by the loss of his Parker pen). Living conforms to the pressures of the car assembly-line where Otto works: he wants to live up to target production, and his loss of self-respect when he is unable to causes him to look for sex in magazines. Ironically, it is not so much this as his poetic, then violent, lament which drives his wife and son out of the house.

Martha is conditioned to believe that each subsequent generation should strive to climb a rung on society's ladder, but Otto, through whose eyes we glimpse the outside world, is content with the security that comes from

To many people's astonishment, the RSC's biggest gamble, following hot on the heels of *The Greeks* was David Edgar's dramatic rendering of *Nicholas Nickleby*. The success of the experiment in marathon total theatre merited a return to the Aldwych for Christmas 1980. When he takes to the boards, Nicholas (Roger Rees) meets an amorous Miss Snevellicci (Suzanne Bertish) and the appalling Infant Phenomenon (Julie Peasgood).

(Photograph by Chris Davies)

co-operating with the speeded-up production schedule at the factory. Like the new German cinema (especially Herzog's *Heart of Glass*) the only saviour from the industrial State is luck; luck, according to Otto, is even responsible for the waiter giving you the right bill.

But with only three characters the play enlarges its themes to include the subjection of women to husbands, and the disenchantments of the younger generation. Ludwig, who is already humiliated at the hands of the state and his friends by being unemployed and penniless for eight months, is further tortured by Otto, who makes his son strip in front of his mother in a futile attempt to find the stolen fifty marks. Martha is alienated by this misuse of authority, and when Otto smashes the flat to pieces, she leaves to find a besdit and a job in order to support herself. Cleaning up the debris in the flat is another scene of reportage: the couple vacuum and sweep in silence until Otto confesses to his own alienation as a worker. Otto likes to conform, so when Martha leaves he is unhappy and tries desperately to forge a triple reconciliation.

Kroetz cleverly exposes the conditioning by TV and industrial economy of the worker's mind: the choice offered is between status and money. Our social conscience makes us ask 'What will X, Y or Z think about what I'm doing,' and from there we desire to remove ourselves from our (self-) imposed situation, a desire for self-recognition and something one can be proud of. Martha can't cope with what she isn't used to; independence is kept at bay by some invisible force about which Kroetz is deliberately vague—expediency? poverty? bordeom? politics? Pick a number . . . any number . . .

(Note: next year GAMBIT will be publishing work by Kroetz in a double volume of recent plays from East and West Germany)

DR

SUNSET by Isaac Babel

(Actor's Soup Kitchen)

Isaac Babel, Russia's greatest short story writer after Chekov, also completed two plays before the Stalinist 1930s impelled him as he put it, to adopt 'the art of silence'. *Marya,* the second of these, made a stunning appearance at the Royal Court in the mid-sixties, whereupon Babel's name promptly vanished from the scene; and it has been left to a group called Actor's Soup Kitchen to launch his first play, *Sunset*.

It is not a straight version of the piece. The director, Helena Kaut-Howson, has supplied a framework from the *Red Cavalry* stories, and my first impression was that she had small chance of successfully combining Babel's close-packed drama of his upbringing in the ghettoes of Odessa with his flinty tales of the 1920 Russo-Polish war. However, a golden rivet has been found in the shape of the story of 'Berestechko', in which the invading Cossacks occupy a village of Polish Jews. The famous irony at the root of Babel's stories was that of a Jew riding with the Cossacks, the Jews' inveterate enemies.

To this, the production adds another and wholly Babelesque irony. Here, in a Jewish strong-hold, the invaders mount an agit-prop performance, written and stage-managed by supply officer Babel, exposing Russo-Jewish society.

Certainly, there is quite enough in *Sunset* to justify the initial device of passing it off as an anti-Semitic fable. Set in the home of the hell-raising old Mendel Krik, a horse-and-dray proprietor who turns every room he enters into a battle-field, the piece records the revenge his sons take on him when he proposes to sell up the business and start a new life with his 20-year-old mistress. His two sons, a gangster and a brutish hussar, simply beat him to a pulp and assume control of the new firm of "Krik and Sons", celebrating this smart move with a grand dinner party where the rabbi gives his official blessing.

A Jewish band strikes up and everyone joins in the dance with the exception of the broken old man seated alone at the head of the table.

This is one of numerous brutally exuberant images, that periodically define the show's meaning.

There is also an extraordinary synagogue scene with the congregation wailing business news in response to a falsetto cantor (Haluk Bilginer), who brings the service to a halt by firing a pistol. 'My contract mentions praying in a synagogue, not a rat hole', he explains. This is actually in the play, but it could equally well be the line of one of the masquerading Cossacks, abruptly resuming his character.

For, as the production develops, the propaganda parable stealthily gives way to a direct parallel between the Jews and the Cossacks, centring on Mendel's loss of his horses, and the theft of a beloved stallion which drives a horse-loving Cossack to resign from the party. And again, the ironies arising from this are fully in key with Babel's own.

The company, led by Christopher Rozycki, Vincenzo Nicoli, and Peter Mathew-Green, excel in the indispensable animal passion and the grotesque. The earlier passages of the show are sometimes blurred; but by the end it achieves a focus of biting, luminous clarity.

Irving Wardle

A SHORT SHARP SHOCK by Howard Brenton & Tony Howard

(Theatre Royal, Stratford; June)

If your play gets a lot of unfavourable (or favourable, depending on your politics) publicity before it's opened, there's a choice to be made: either you make sure you live up to expectations, or else you live down the nonsense that has been talked about it. *A Short Sharp Shock*—forecast by its opponents as a savage anti-governmental threat—turned out to be a very flaccid and not very funny political satire. Oh yes! the members of the cabinet *were* played by women, I'll grant you that . . . but no fool could see why. Gwen Taylor was a close simulacrum of our real-life leaderene, and the part was stronger by dint of that: 'It's only 4am,' she drawls, 'shall we make some cuts?' Images, of which there are many, tend to be unnecessarily surreal: the set is flanked by a gigantic tank (pigeons on its gun barrel) on one side and a living room with sky walls on the other. In the middle sat a paper maché pig. At one point it came close to meeting its bovine counterpart.

So, in the absence of imagery, make the images surreal, but the tirades were boring cant. Theatre reflects life, if you like, but if we're going to be interested/engaged/entertained or what have you, there's got to be some selective anamorphosis. Keith Joseph gets on my nerves, but an ersatz Keith Joseph haranguing me from a stage gets on my nerves absolutely. The message is plain—we didn't need to enter the theatre to know what that was—so what else are the authors saying? Jumpcutting from windy rhetoric to eccentric cartoon cut-outs isn't going to satisfy an audience's search for 'revelation', and it's tangoing on the cliff edge at the Blackpool conference to give the only credible role to the dreadful Thatch. And whilst I have perhaps come to doubt the political acuity of Mr Bruce Forsyth, I reckon you'd get more laughs watching *The Generation Game*.

DR

THE FATTED CALF by Jeremy Sandford

(ICA; June 1980)

We were forewarned about the 'surrealist' style of presentation, and had advance notice of a play that somehow tried to explore the 'metaphysics' of prostitution. But there was too much dampness for the 'deeply expressed emotions and explosive symbolism' (as Crystal Theatre director, P.B. Davies put it) to detonate, and Sandford's technique of collated vignettes (some of which were quite amusing) did little to give a coherent picture of anything. This revue-type format might have

Robert Hamilton as Otto, Rachel Bell as Martha in *Tom Fool* by Franz Xavier
Kroetz at the Half Moon Theatre.　　　(Photograph by Jane Harper)

Sunset by Isaac Babel　　　(Photograph by Roger de Wolf)

succeeded had the playwright been content to treat the subject matter, if not as a joke, at least with tongue in cheek. Surrealism, on the other hand, and metaphysics (whatever that is) are generally speaking quite serious topics, too serious, if anything, to sully themselves with anything so banal as a charter for prostitutes, or a Whores' Union. The idea is not so far-fetched; author Sandford himself has had experience in getting such a thing off the ground, and I don't mean that metaphysically. Yet spliced in among the pages of documentary, no doubt faithfully copied out from the author's book, *Prostitutes*, which in turn are interspersed with little comic sketches and symbolist tableaux (a female Christ doing the stations of the cross in Ann Summers gear, beaten by a burly actor in a hangman's hood and a blue bathing costume), is a long tirade—presumably the point of it all—where the cast lobbies the audience for reform of the law. Not entirely the most convincing presentation of a serious argument, if such it be. But Sandford's other point—more of an observation really—that a prostitute is meant to sell not sex, but her own degradation, was more illuminating and more subtle, as I wish the play had been.

DG

BURIED CHILD by Sam Shepard

(Hampstead; June 1980)

There's some clever patterning and a nice dose of laughs in this moody, lugubrious comedy about a homecoming gone wrong. Pa is an invalid, glued to his sofa, pills, whisky and TV set; Ma reminisces upstairs about young men who took her to the races while dressing for Sunday service where the minister seems to be in line for some servicing himself; Tilden is the elder son hiding from some mysterious trouble far away in New Mexico, who keeps entering with moronic singlemindedness bearing armfuls of vegetables that have mysteriously begun to sprout in the Illinois rain; and Bradley is the one-legged barber who comes in to shave his dad's head while the old man sleeps.

It's the grandson, Vince, who comes 'home' to all this, a world he poorly remembers, and which his spunky girlfriend finds a bit too eerie for comfort. The family, for their part, do not remember him at all, not even his father. Much of this reads like cruising with Harold Pinter in a Chevy down Route 66, or an evening with the Glums *á l'américaine*, apart, that is, from subterranean rumours and rumblings deep down the bunghole of memory. Ma, it seems, once had a baby by another man (her own son? or am I on the wrong tack?) which Pa simply drowned and buried in the garden. All these years the family has lived with the secret, until Pa suddenly decides to divulge it to his grandson's girlfriend Shelly, for no reason I could fathom. She eventually leaves Vince who inherits the house (as a prize for his determination to rediscover his own roots?) and decides to stay to 'continue' the line.

93

Speaking of lines, there are fewer funny ones than funny contexts. As Shelly clutches Bradley's prosthetic leg in self-protection from his menaces, Ma bellows over his whimpering: 'You give my son back his leg, you hear me?' while the priest who only came in for 'a spot of tea' stands there hopelessly, a bouquet of roses in his arms. As Bradley's whimpering turns into bawling, she turns on him, 'You don't need your leg right now so just shut up!' Well, I thought it was funny at the time.

In the end Pa seems to get buried under a blanket while Tilden is out in the back lot digging up not carrots or corn this time, but the long-buried infant (his own?) which, cradling in his arms he carries back upstairs to his Ma, as the lights dim to blackout. What happens next is left to our imagination. The moment is well-prepared, dramatically, and produces the right kind of frisson. Is that what they give the Pulitzer Prize for nowadays?

(Shucks, well mebbe they do. No stars for this production, though, in spite of a fine set from Gemma Jackson. Perhaps director Nancy Meckler found it hard to explain to the cast what they were supposed to be doing.)

DG

COMMITMENTS by Dusty Hughes

(Bush Theatre; June 1980)

Dusty Hughes' latest is like one of those narrative paintings of an historic moment in which the artist gets all the colours and expressions perfect to a T while the action flounders like a neurotic hieroglyph, pregnant with meaning and yet helpless to divulge it. The moments here in question might one day seem more momentous than momentary—and they certainly did back then when the miners' strike and the three-day-week seemed to be driving Britain to that ineluctable precipice where finally class war is declared. Hughes' re-run adopts the optic perspective of the extreme left, fomenting their revolutionary foam in Hugh's Earls Court flat. Hugh (Alan Rickman) is one of those bourgeois intellectuals you read so much about in Pravda; you know the kind I mean, he's got Kapital by heart yet there's a Porsche parked in his drive. While Claire (Paola Dionisotti) is off doing a sort of musical Vanessa Redgrave act, playing the part I might add with the right sort of fire and drive, Hugh suddenly abandons Yevtushenko and Snow for the wintry labour of revolutionary agitation in her RSP/WRP organization. We never learn much about what finally sickens him and weans him off political involvement, though in the interim there is a fair show with a fair deal of witty banter, all of which I must say I enjoyed. (Ay, yes, it brought back memories . . .) The opening moments of the play allowed us to listen in to one of those familiar old voices I didn't recognize, reminiscing about the early days of the Bolshevik Revolution. 'Blessed,' he said, 'was it then to be alive.' Perhaps Hughes wished to make some comment about the nostalgia of extreme-left organisations for the irrevocable ethers of 'real' revolutionism. I don't know. If so,

94

couldn't he have offered a perspective a bit wider and less clever round the edges? The passing of time has left few of us any wiser than once we were, and the political situation is, if anything, even more stagnant.

DG

A LESSON FROM ALOES by Athol Fugard
(Cottesloe; July 1980)

Is it just an illusion or is it true that nowadays you've got to go to the Third World if you want to find plays dealing with the grand old themes of human dignity, courage, betrayal? There must be a lesson for us in Fugard's *Aloes,* though it isn't very clear whether South Africa rates as the Third World. Treading familiar ground of white man's guilt, Fugard misses the quagmire of liberal attitudes. Peter's wife, Gladys, was never a sympathizer of the Cause, as she sardonically phrases it, yet she too has suffered from the totalitarian regime. Hers I felt to be a more challenging symbol than Peter's aloes, a kind of cactus indigenous to this trying land and which he fondly collects and names, now that humans have deserted him. For her privacy has, literally, been violated: her diaries, inventories of her meagre sense of self, have been sequestrated by the arbitrary hand of Broeder justice, and now, one nervous breakdown later, she's got nothing left from which to build. English, but native-born, her ties to the land are less strong than her husband's. So, indeed, are those of the coloured militant, Steve, whom he has been accused of informing on, and who now (after being banned for three years) is packing up for England. Why not, he asks bitterly, 'in England we can sit and talk as much as we like. That's all we ever did here.'

All this comes out, slowly, in dribs and drabs. The politics and lost ideals, the wounds and that awful form of despair that creeps up on people who have ceased to live beyond the level of survival. Gladys' schizoid traits show up nicely, showing how those who have suffered most are often driven by a curious quirk of human nature into reactionary attitudes. 'Is there nothing gentle in your world?' she shrieks at him, like a finger on the rim of a glass, 'You have a perverse need of dwelling on what is ugly about this country.' They are sitting in the garden, waiting for Steve to arrive for dinner, waiting in the sun that is too strong for English skin, and too harsh for poorer Afrikaaner farmers such as Peter used to be. Only the aloes, all thorns and bitterness but with an unpredictable propensity to flower in the most unlikely places have adapted successfully; Is there a parable here, an image of the indigenous black population who were significantly absent from this stage? Fugard's visiting Market Theatre production perversely dwells on something very ugly about South Africa, and that is the impotence of those who wish to see things change. Though tending to plod a little, the pressure is never relaxed, and no easy answers are offered. Depressing, really. But it's cheering to know that there are Afrikaners and English South Africans who do not sleep easily at night. Provided, of course, that it's true.

DG

WATCH ON THE RHINE by Lillian Hellman
(National Theatre)

I liked *Watch on the Rhine*. Now, among other reviewers this was an unfashionable attitude. Critical of the play's glib stage murder, of its lack of reality, of its bad construction, of its standard drawing-room mechanisms, they dismissed it as a flawed, old-fashioned masterpiece. But in its original Aldwych production in 1942 it ran for 673 performances. It is a play which retains an astonishingly modern impact despite its anti-fascist subject—the protection by American sympathizers of a non-Nazi wartime German emigré. If it does tend at times towards the mawkishly sentimental, the slush didn't conceal the pain of loyalty or a Peggy Ashcroft stoicism which never tips over into the arch. Sentimentalizing is, when all's said and done, the logistic of propaganda. Breaking the audience's heart with goodness amounts to agitprop done without compromise but with . . . ah yes . . . the word is 'taste'.

DR

THE ELEPHANT MAN by Bernard Pomerance
(Lyttleton; July 1980)

A bizarre play with a bizarre stage history, Pomerance's *Elephant* had to go for a stroll on Broadway before Londoners could find time to give it a second look. My hand goes up to plead the excuse that I was elsewhere at the time, while others in this sorry business seek to justify their initial displeasure. Roland Rees' new production for the NT is a triumphant return, and a *tour de force* is David Schofield's performance as the hideously deformed sideshow freak who is given a reprieve from the horrors inflicted on him by his 'fellows', thanks to the intervention of scientist Sir Frederick Treves. Rationalist philanthropy may well have been the motive in his own mind, but Pomerance's play opens up an intriguing area of debate by challenging and **demystifying** the very notion of charity, probing not simply latent or unconscious motives, but the reciprocal relationship between helper and helped as well.

The play covers the last four, relatively edenic, years of John Merrick's life, under Treves' good care at the London Hospital. Fed and sheltered, protected and given the opportunity to educate himself, Merrick soon shows that in spite of his grotesque appearance ('the head of a misshapen mass of cauliflower-like growths; great bosses protruding from his forehead; spongy, fungus-looking skin; a bulbous inverted upper lip; pendulous folds of skin hanging from chest and back') he is nevertheless a sentient, witty and intelligent man. Soon it becomes fashionable in Society to be seen to show pity for him, and Merrick's London Hospital room becomes a salon in which he receives and entertains the 'best people'. Treves' plan to help him to live as normal a life as possible seems to be working, though the 'best people' bring as presents cigarettes he cannot smoke, hairbrushes and walking sticks that are hideously inappropriate.

'Props,' says the only one of his visitors who seems to show some authentic interest, actress Mrs Kendal. For isn't this (much applauded) aspiration to normalcy a yearning to be sham, to play a role? His visitors, indeed, polish him like a glass to see some flattering part of themselves reflected in him, while underneath all somehow feel with discomfort the stirrings of another monster, a private and moral one, the underside of Victorian privilege and hypocrisy. Merrick's condition actually worsens as he moves nearer to the rest of us, while Treves, 'incapable of distinguishing between the charitable act and the assertion of [his own] authority,' founders in the moral swamp of his society's values. Isn't this but another form of voyeurism, another form of exploitation, of a more subtle, insidious variety? Merrick helps Treves get recognition, a knighthood and funds for the London Hospital. Pomerance's vignettish but focused text and Rees' non-naturalistic production (no make-up for the Elephant Man, Schofield does it with his body—and it works) probe this rich if murky area, pulling out many a plum. The deformed emerge in a clearer light, as the mirror of the 'normal', reflecting the transcendant smile of humanist ethics and so confirming us; parodying and exhibiting our guilts, fears, anxieties, and so mocking and disturbing us. Poor monster, he just wanted to be like everyone else.

DG

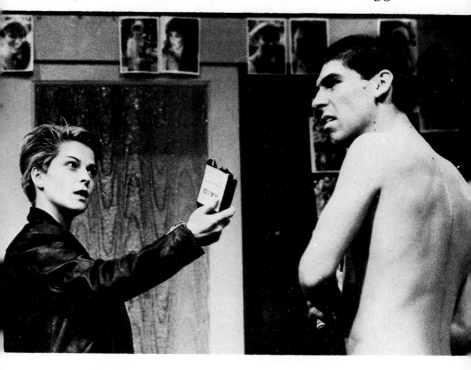

Toyah Willcox and Daniel Peacock in *Sugar and Spice* by Nigel Williams at the Royal Court Theatre. Once again it seemed as though Williams' overrich verbal mixture might flood the play's racing carburettor. The play is published by Eyre Methuen.   (Photograph by John Haynes)

Hailed as one of the greatest triumphs of the fringe's recent swing from east to west (ends), *Pal Joey* saw the musical début of Sian Phillips. The Rodgers and Hart show had its first London revival in 25 years under the careful guidance of Half Moon director Rob Walker. Denis Lawson plays the eponymous loser. (Photograph by John Haynes)

DE SOFTIES

(Oval House)

I have never thought that the combination of pop and live theatre can be a happy one; you always expect more of one than the other, and if you don't get fed up with the first . . . well . . . But that was until I discovered De Softies (which apparently means straight men who prefer the company of gays—a rare generic form this side of Harwich), who are an energetic Dutch beat group, best summed-up as Amsterdam's very gay answer to the Baron Knights.

It is a show of undiluted madness, with three men singing episodes on a journey from city gloom to celebratory gaiety. The stations of the cross are marked by relationships, macho encounters in the US, Sicilian boys and holidays in the south of France. Catchy toons sometimes slip in—and calypsos, ballads and Johnny Halliday bounce make welcome breaks from the tonally monotonous soft-rock. Visually it's a cramped experience; the background slides are professionally handled but performers can only make up in range what they lack in depth. If you're feeling low, you'll be shaken up. Entertainment? Boy . . . do we all need it now!

DR

BODY POLITIC by Moving Being

(ICA; Oct 1980)

Almost since their beginnings I have followed the work of Moving Being, and I suppose I have seen virtually all of their productions. There are now five members, where once there were six—and the incumbents change as regularly as the style. It seems, though, as if there has been a conscious return to director Geoff Moore's first love: the multi-media performance with a keen use of video, film, back-projection and recorded sound. With such a multiplicity of background material, what actor can hope to transcend the audience's vision of pure artifice despite the honest attempt to mix Blake and anger in constructing an informative collage . . .

DR

DREAMER by Bill Colvill

(Half Moon; Nov 1980)

Not content with *Pal Joey*—which was a success—the Half Moon put their money on a modern East-End musical—which wasn't. Wasn't a success and wasn't a modern musical. On a story that is a simplistic mercantile version of King Lear (exiled son instead of daughter) are woven some hybrid songs—which at times proved beyond the talents of the singers—and a tatty love story with political sentiments. Perhaps the worthiest thing about it is the motif: the individualist bosses fighting the Bengali sewing-workers collectivism—but handled so naively as to be insulting. *Dreamer* managed to be both garish **and** slow-paced; the format was old-fashioned and the stage work was, on the whole, just not interesting enough to make up for the rambling, picaresque plot. Next time an East End musical about punks, skinheads and the National Front might make a lot more sense.

DR

THIS JOCKEY DRIVES LATE NIGHTS by Henry Livings
(Theatre Royal, Stratford East)

Henry Livings claims that his latest play borrows its formula—the inevitability of man's obligation to his work—from Tolstoy's *Power of Darkness*, a study of the pressures of farming on the Kulak peasants. Be that as it may, *This Jockey Drives Late Nights* was the play of 1980 which—although a disaster—came nearest to success. Unfortunately it got far too clever for itself, far too long for its own good (and ours) and couldn't make up its mind between melodrama and grotesque farce. Briefly it is a tale of disaster for Nick the romeo mechanic in a mini-cab company. After the owner is dispatched to an early grave, Nick marries the widow but flirts with the daughter, who, giving birth on the day she should be getting married, has her baby buried alive by father Nick. Although some of the dialogue is stagey, it was thanks to the actors that it was saved from lack of credibility and the over-epigrammatic. In effect, it is an Oedipus story grafted onto an uncontrollable machismo which is eventually subjugated—at great emotional cost—by some machiavellian mothers and wives. The ending is retribution and recrimination with all the purity of a Victorian penny-dreadful. Sadly, farce with serious undertones remains the unchallenged rutting ground of head-hunter Orton.

DR

TELEVISION TIMES by Peter Prince
(RSC Warehouse; December 1980)

If a play about fishing can avoid drawing a largely piscatorial public, why should a play about television appeal mainly to insiders? Outsiders, of course, prefer the cosy media-wrapped image they know and love to the sordid truths which Peter Prince would have us believe lie behind our silver screens. Any curiosity about the insiders' world would have been satisfied by *Television Times:* it is a bitty, bitter and bitchy summary of a group of caricatures who perform guignolesque humanoid acts of nastiness on each other in the race to success.

Television is the child that was 'born in the age we live in.' And yet nothing could distort reality more successfully than the camera-eye: the old are made to look young, the sad are made to look funny, and manqué film directors are made to look like people who have ideas. Well, TV fiction may be stranger than fact, but I for one am tired of watching plays that don't try to reach out and shake every member of the audience by the mood tubes.

DR

NOT QUITE JERUSALEM by Paul Kember
(Royal Court; December 1980)

A new play about four young working-class Englanders seeking sun, sand and sex on a kibbutz might not have you racing off to the Royal Court— but it should. For if you go down to Sloane Square today you'll never believe your eyes; the idiot-level (and therefore excusable?) anti-semitism you see on stage will actually make you laugh . . . helplessly and in spite of yourself. Paul Kember charts the cultural divide between the hard-working, enthusiastic and optimist kibbutzniks and their volunteer visitors escaping from strike-bound, new-town, run-down Blighty. The English can't find where to lay the blame for their apathy until one of them articulates their Angst in order to save the day. This is Mike, an idyll-seeking Cambridge drop-out, the one character who mars an otherwise perfect play; the tone of his freedom-fighter worthiness and his self-sacrificing defence stick in the throat more than the whingeing pleas of his fellow countrymen who have got themselves into trouble and risk expulsion from the camp.

Much of what he diagnoses as the English malaise is beyond criticism—an accurate portrait as such stage-portraits go, but never let it be said that the kibbutz is the only way forward . . . it looks more like a receiving ground for failures and misfits and anyone disgusted by the class system. But it's naive to expect the eloquent middle-classes to become the mouthpiece of the workers and failures; even the play proudly denies that they can ever come together in some common patriotism. Still, any writer who dares to say that it's better to stand up and defend eccentricity than try to run away deserves to be heard . . . and heard . . . and heard.

DR

LOOT by Joe Orton
(Lyric Studio; Arts Theatre)

By the time *Loot* was first performed in February 1965, the play had undergone several censoral changes, including one or two scenes of questionable taste. The latest production (transferred to the Arts Theatre) is directed by

101

Kenneth Williams, Orton's long-time friend. Williams has tried to bring us 'the production Orton intended', replacing original scenes and language which add force to this ferocious attack on the law and the church. Indeed the production has a feeling of strong empathy between director and writer. The play's central character, the psychopathic police inspector Truscott is brought to horrible life by John Malcolm, looking like a maniacal Inspector Lockhart.

As farce, *Loot* is a fine example of Orton's continued preoccupation with the old fashioned comic commodities: prostitution, adultery, rape. In his own words, 'farce is higher than comedy in that it is very close to tragedy.' Here, the tragic themes are death and corruption, the latter expertly personified by Truscott ('Is that an anagram?') and Fay (Joan Blackham), the late Mrs McLeavy's nurse who helps Hal and Dennis (Rory Edwards, Philip Martin Brown) hide their ill-gotten gains in the mother's coffin.

Williams' direction is almost literally bulging with inuendo and provocative sexual anomaly; it's provocative in more ways than one, of course, and would not have withstood the test of time so well if it had not been that the play's main attack is on the British public's unquestioning faith in its law enforcers. In that respect, *Loot* is more relevant today than it has ever been.

T. Sessions

Olivier Pierre and Susan Hampshire in *The Revolt*, a production which, it was hoped, would help the New End's sticky finances.

(Photograph by Lesley Hamilton)

THE REVOLT by Villiers de l'Isle Adam; directed by Simone Benmussa

(Hampstead; Dec 1980)

The set is stark. Large square windows look out onto a dark winter forest. The stage rises to the back where there is an armchair, a desk to stage-right and in the foreground a wrought-iron gateway; to the left a booth-like lobby. The window, the floors, the iron-work are painted black—the symbolic rendition of a middle-class French home of the late 19th century—and the play sets out to communicate in similarly evocative terms the austerity and deathly coldness of the relationships that have both constructed and inhabit this world. The problem, for a contemporary audience, is that in terms of austerity and coldness, this is a world largely gone by. Again (as in Peter Nichols' *Passion Play*) we are confronted with a woman (Susan Hampshire) who leaves her home and husband (Olivier Pierre), only this time not for what he has done, but for what he has not: he has not loved. She longs for warmth, poetry, life. He offers only a rather matter-of-fact, statistical, business-like attitude, completely devoid of passion, which he regards only as a kind of dreaming or madness. His wife is merely a piece of the mundane jigsaw that defines his view of life.

The strength of the play is that each viewpoint is rendered with conviction, and some of its more successful moments derive from the husband's complete (and honest) misunderstanding of the wife's feelings of repression. A weakness is that, like the set, the characters and too many of their lines are painted in this stark contrast where the worlds of poetry and reason are made to seem somewhat irreconcilable. Certainly their lives are intended to appear tangential, but when the wife, having walked out, returns in a mood of defeat and resignation to tell her husband 'We have nothing to discuss,' one feels there is both the point and the pointlessness of the play.

A modern audience will naturally sympathize with the woman's longings, but dramatically the dice are too heavily loaded, and the male character somewhat under-written. If there is to be a debate between passionate poetry and cold reasoning, should it not be fought out more completely, so that we glimpse some common ground, some hint of resolution? Simply to leave everything in the tangential void at which we started states the question poetically, but does not involve the audience dramatically. Given these limitations, the acting and direction were well-paced and succeeded in evolving a suitable atmosphere. Susan Hampshire bore the look and manner of one proud in defeat. Olivier Pierre captured precisely the uncomprehending logic of a complacent man suddenly thrown into confusion by a passion he has never felt, and therefore cannot understand. *The Revolt* finally comes across as a play for its own time, which in our time can only re-state questions that, unless we suffer from the complacency of the play's 'husband', are already very apparent.

MB

PASSION PLAY by Peter Nichols

(RSC, Aldwych; Jan 1981)

Middle-aged married man is seduced by voluptuous young female photographer. There is a protracted relationship. Wife can't handle it; goes to psychiatrist; attempts suicide; eventually walks out of home in the religious season of Christmas. The scenario is hackneyed, but Peter Nichols builds the play with some very fine, very delicate observations on the theme of human duplicity. For instance, even when certain characters appear, ostensibly, at their most honest, there is often an ulterior motive at work: it is through the wife (Billie Whitelaw) that the girl (Louise Jameson) informs the husband (Benjamin Whitrow) of her attraction to him, in assumed flippancy; the wife's best friend informs her of her husband's secret affair 'for her own good'; the husband sends his wife to a psychiatrist whom he knows to be sympathetic to male prejudice.

Accompanying the detailed observation is a sharp sense of humour, with more than a handful of good one-liners. The central device of introducing the alter-egos or consciences of the wife and husband in the form of another actor and actress (Anton Rodgers and Eileen Atkins) gives rise to several comic situations wherein the 'false' and 'true' attitudes are juxtaposed, often with brutal candour. However, whereas the roles are clearly distinguished in the first act, which is also lighter in mood (almost a Laingian sit-com), they become muddied in the more serious second act; the 'true' husband or wife often taking over the public role, as in the psychiatrist or suicide scenes. The technique is not particularly original—it is reminiscent of the balcony scene in Woody Allen's *Annie Hall*, and (in the sense of a 'spirit' actor on stage unseen by other characters) of Coward's *Blithe Spirit*. However, the former is sensibly short, the latter intelligibly consistent, Mr Nichols' use seems sometimes overstretched and indistinct.

Passion Play arrives at no particular conclusion, wisely relying on the situations it so well depicts to offer the audience however much truth they are able to take. Still, the characters will strike many as somewhat dated in their concerns. Can we really sympathize with a wife who only wants to know, 'How can I keep him?' or with a husband whose only means of creating new relationships is to lie and cheat? Can we really care for two people who seem so completely wrapped up in themselves? If the ethos of the play takes us back to the fifties, we can go even farther back for a balanced view of such affairs, to John Donne's poem *Confined Love:*

Who e'r rigg'd faire ship to lie in harbors,
And not to seek new lands, or not to deal withall?
Or built faire houses, set trees, and arbors,
Only to lock up, or else let them fall?
Good is not good, unlesse
A thousand it possesse,
But doth wast with greedinesse.

The acting is very fine by all concerned, as true to the words as the words are true to the situations. But just as the characters make no connection of their problems to a larger, social world, neither does the play. We are left to draw our own conclusions. And what conclusions dare the middle-aged married couple draw, I wonder?

MB

Royal Scottish Academy of Music & Drama

School of Drama

Diploma in Dramatic Art

A 3 year course in professional acting for stage TV and radio. This course is accredited by the National Council for Drama Training and the School of Drama is a member of the Conference of Drama Schools

Diploma in Speech and Drama

A 3 year course in educational and community drama. Discussions are now in progress with the Scottish Education Department and the University of Glasgow for this diploma to be validated by the university as a BA (Dramatic Studies). It is hoped that the first intake to this degree may be admitted in 1981

Technical Certificate

A 1 year course in technical aspects of theatre and TV

Entry to all courses is by interview, plus audition for the diploma courses, held in February, April, May and July each year

Prospectus giving detailed information is available from the Secretary, School of Drama, Royal Scottish Academy of Music & Drama, St George's Place, Glasgow G2 1BS. Tel 041-332 5294.

EUROPALIA 80: The Face Behind The Mask
Anne-Marie Glasheen

One hundred and fifty years ago Belgium was born—the lands and the people had always been there, but 1830 saw the birth of the State. In 1943—through necessity as the French touring theatrical companies had been stopped by the occupying Germans, Claude Etienne founded the theatre called *Le Rideau de Bruxelles*. It opened with a play by the young and unknown playwright Georges Sion: *La Matronne d'Ephèse*. In 1948, Claude Etienne, walking down the corridors of the Palais des Beaux Arts, bumped into the newly appointed Secretary General, Paul Willems. He asked him: 'Are you related to Paul Willems?' To which came the reply: 'I am Paul Willems.' 'Write me a play then, will you, I liked your novels!'

In 1980 Le Rideau de Bruxelles is one of Belgium's leading theatres, with Claude Etienne still running the show. The Europalia Festival was dedicated to Belgium in 1980, its sesquicentenary. Europalia—always devoted to one of the member states of the EEC—is the brainchild of the now Director of the Palais des Beaux Arts, Paul Willems, also by now the author of some twelve plays.

Brussels was definitely not the same city I had visited last year. Apart from the unbelievable daily queues for the Breughel exhibition outside the Palais des Beaux Arts, the city was buzzing with activity and excitement; and a feeling of awareness of itself—in that awareness was also a sense of pride. The city was a host and it was dressed to please— clean, wearing its autumn clothes and scattering like rose petals, golden leaves at the feet of its visitors.

The first play I saw, was *L'Ange Couteau,* the latest work by Jean Sigrid, who, though he has been writing plays since the war, has only in recent years been receiving the recognition he deserves. The play itself was good—the story of a man organising and attending his granddaughter's wedding reception. The young man responsible for the serving of the drinks and the cleaning up wants to be adopted into the family as the man's grandson. From the beginning there is the feeling that fate is leading the solitary figure of the grandfather to his inevitable end, and that the young man is the messenger of fate. The play is rich in dreams, reminiscences, regrets and a vision of the next world. In parts it is very surrealistic and as the drama progresses, the role of the harpy-like cleaners develops and the play is taken to its ultimate conclusion with the grandfather dead, but still communicating with his adopted grandson.

Georges Sion's *La Matronne d'Ephèse* surprised me, as I expected it to be very dated. In fact it was incredibly funny. The language was racy and the acting superb, especially as timing was all important. A widow in Ancient Greece, as a show of love for her recently departed husband, decides she must make the ultimate sacrifice. She and a friend, who will share her sacrifice, sit in his tomb, to starve themselves to death. But she falls in love—slowly but surely—with a soldier who by chance stumbles in. He is supposed to be guarding the body of a hanged man—were this to disappear, he would have to take its place. However it does get stolen, and to show her love, the woman allows the soldier to replace the body with that of her husband—it is *he* who makes the final sacrifice. It was not the sort of play to ever radically change anyone's life, but it was after all the play that had sparked off the modern Belgian theatrical movement.

It is a feat in itself to attempt to produce Maeterlinck's *L'Oiseau Bleu,* for there are eighty characters and ten scene changes. The fact that Thierry Salmon attempted it with only twenty five actors is to be applauded regardless of anything else. It is actually a play for children aged from seven to seventy, and should perhaps be done as a pantomime with the baddies being hissed, and a few men dressed up as women.

Maeterlinck was again on the menu the following evening—but as the main course, rather than the dessert. Monique Dorsel at her Théâtre Poème, as a reaction to the move to body theatre has gone back to text rather than performance; and theatricalizes them. In *Les Serres Chaudes,* she had taken a collection of Maeterlinck's poems, and together with four other actresses, took us on a journey through his tortured soul, his fantasies, fear of the abyss, grotesque visions and dreams. The obsession with illness, suffering and death that mars beauty, corrupts purity and distorts sensual pleasure. One was plunged into one's own subconscious, trapped and accused by Maeterlinck's words. The poems were heavy with religious imagery—the Jesuits had done their work well with his soul—eternal damnation was his greatest fear. The visions evoked were the ones Bosch and Breughel had seen, and that Crommelynck and de Ghelderode, as well as contemporary writers would and did evoke, from deep inside themselves. The five women in their tattered robes, came into the theatre's cafe like ghosts to lead you in by the hand—into a 'hot house' to be trapped and suffocated by the heat, pain and suffering. Then you are led, again by the actresses, to a bigger room, more verbal visions and anguished torture of the soul. In the third room, after clambering over rags, you sit. And if the words are not enough they put the ragged sheets that are on the floor, over your heads—your head goes through a hole in the sheet. You are trapped now, and the actresses go round staring at you through the rags suspended from the ceiling accusing you with their eyes and words, disappearing and reappearing like ghosts. A cathartic experience.

There was a complete contrast in Paul Willems' *La Ville à Voile—*
superbly acted and brilliantly directed by Henri Ronse. The Russians
found themselves in Stanislavski, the French in Barrault . . . and the
Belgians have found themselves in Ronse. Having worked in Paris for
ten years, Henri Ronse has come back to Belgium to his roots; sure of
himself and his identity. He needed to distance himself from Belgium to
do this. He feels that at the present time, Belgian culture, Belgian
sensitivities are threatened from within. Threatened by politicians, by
opportunitists and by those bent on dividing Belgium. He feels that
the time has come to reaffirm Belgium's cultural identity and to
transfer to the theatre, 'the gold of Belgium's dreams, the light of
its skies and the light of its thoughts.' I went to a rehearsal of
Maeterlinck's *Les Aveugles,* and saw Ronse at work. He cuts a very
Balzacien figure in his academic gown-like smock, white scarf, round
glasses and ample frame, dedicated to his task in life, identifying and
exposing Belgian theatre to the world. He feels that Paul Willems
complements Maeterlinck, and he likes alternating from one to the
other. In Willems' plays he works out from the characters: in
Maeterlinck's he works from the structure of the play in to the characters.
He hopes that his new theatre–Le Nouveau Théâtre de Belgique–will
make of Brussels the centre of European artistic creativity that it was at
the time of the Symbolists and Surrealists.

La Ville a Voile is about Josty, who at seventeen, stows away to Borneo,
with not a penny to his name, where he makes his fortune. Forty years
later, he returns to Antwerp, rich, ready to buy the happiness that had
always eluded him. But everything has changed: the woman he loved has
aged, the shop across the road from where he used to sleep on the pavement
as a boy, which he has now bought; no longer contains all the objects
that used to be there. His friends speak empty, meaningless phrases and
the girls, though still beautiful, belong to a different generation. It is
the story of a man who, loving life, is near to death, and sees all his dreams
disappear out of his reach. Josty is torn apart by the cruelty of fate and
escapes back to Borneo to dream of the Antwerp he had wanted to find.
The production was an inspired stroke of genius. From the ceiling hung
huge sails that could be raised and lowered. And in the same way that
he had got Delvaux to paint the scenery for *Les Amants Puérils,* so Ronse
used Magritte's paintings to reinforce the main themes.

Giant plastic bags next in Frederic Flamand's *Quarantaine.* This was pure
body theatre, not a word throughout the whole fifty minutes, just the
rhythmic repetitive sound of the amplified fiddle. The actors follow this
music with strange jerky movements, each trapped at the beginning in a
cylinder or bubble of plastic. Released, the actors play in the air with
lights, then suddenly one actor comes on with a cauldron on his head and
empty sleeves hanging from his hips, another dragging a long copper pipe,
another with a sort of bottomless cauldron round his waist. They break
into a rather grotesque dance, drumming thimbled fingers on the metal
around them: effective, if only for its reference to paintings by

Jérôme Bosch. There then follow a fire and water ritual, a kind of torture. At the end, then, a kind of hell or purgatory of the trapped soul, unable to reach out and communicate, a kind of primitive dance.

Paul Willems' *Il Pleut dans ma Maison* had first been performed in 1962. But it did not seem to date. The production, like the play, was timeless. This is Willems' best known play and tickets are always sold out. Passage into the auditorium was through dead leaves that had been strewn on the ground, and under the torn umbrellas suspended from the ceiling. No stage curtain, just some fine netting with trees painted on gave the feeling that actors, audience, stage, auditorium were practically interchangeable. Like Alice, we were about to go through the looking glass—but which side were we on to begin with? The play is about a young woman who inherits a house. She arrives to find a tree growing in the house, the windows broken to let in the breeze and the stairs and beds a playground for errant raindrops. The guardians of the house see nothing extraordinary in this and are horrified that she wants to sell it. They persuade her to let them advertise it as a luxury hotel—a hotel offering all that modern technological life deprives humanity of, a hotel suspended in time and space. But things go wrong, a relative returns from the past and sends a couple of the living temporarily into the next world. The young lady's fiancé arrives and is won over by the opposition, a recently married couple arrive and buy the house, prompting an assassination attempt on them. In the end the dead return to where they belong, and the living come back to live, we presume, happily ever after, in this topsy turvy world, fishing for the reflections of weeping willows and clouds, and setting traps to catch sounds for their 'sound fountain'. What is reality and what is fantasy does not matter, the play is a mirror, a reflection where the impossible is the norm, and reality unthinkable.

Those ten days in Brussels were to prove that the theatrical movement over there is an interesting and developing one. Belgium's theatrical tradition has its roots firmly planted in Belgian soil and the sap is rising from it to nourish the activity of its various branches. It is attracting not only interest, but actors, musicians and directors from all over the world. Even the Belgians themselves are aware of it. The monsters of Belgium's deep unconscious, first glimpsed by Bosch and Breughel, are still there, not only in the paint but in the words, through Maeterlinck, Magritte, Crommelynck and de Ghelderode to Delvaux, Willems and Sigrid. The creative sensibility of Belgians is permeated with, at the same time, a sensuality and a morbidity. There is the feeling that two parallel words are overlapping, but that each is unaware of the other, being only concerned with its own inner dream. Time and space are suspended and out of step with one another. It is what is not there that is the threat, not what is there. Hence a preoccupation with dreams, fantasy and the fantastic, and an obsession with mirrors and all that reflects in an attempt to identify one of those unknowns—oneself. But all you see in the mirror is the back of your head.

REVIEWS OF BOOKS

JUST PLAY: BECKETT'S THEATER by Ruby Cohn
(Princeton University Press; 313pp; £10.20)

I have always been of the opinion that the critic is a sort of larval thing
condemned never to become a fly, perhaps the image of Beckett's Worm,
through whom others talk. The critic must make his meal of other people's
words, and worse than that, he must use himself as a kind of agent of
semantic transformation, like the Indian mother chewing meat in her own
mouth before passing it to Baby. Neither metaphor is perhaps felicitous,
but Baby still wants to know when books about Beckett will start tasting
of Beckett and not of American College Professors, as so many do.

Ruby Cohn (Professor of Comparative Drama at UCLA) has written
several books on Beckett and is (along with John Fletcher, Richard Coe,
James Knowlson, and others) one of the Superworms at the top of the hill.
She claims to have actually attended the first production of *En attendant
Godot* in Paris in 1953, and her latest book has the virtue of being fully
up-to-date with recent developments and discoveries in Beckett criticism
(such as the **first** version of *Endgame,* Knowlson's work on Beckett's
production notes for *Krapp's Last Tape,* as well as ten pages of a jettisoned
play—*Human Wishes* (1937), which Professor Cohn has received permission
to print.) Another virtue of this work is the section devoted to directors
of Beckett's work and their approaches, to adaptations of prose texts to
the stage, and to Beckett's own work as a producer of his plays. Professor
Cohn does not hesitate to express her own tastes and preferences here, and
this part of the book is generally well-informed and quite readable.

Indeed, her approach to Beckett's work has undergone a number of
changes since she first began to write about the man. In *Back to Beckett*
she herself testified to a certain interpretative presumptuousness which
had marked the earlier *The Comic Gamut,* and which she felt she had
eliminated (though to my mind the one was a rehash of the other without
the gravy). *Just Play* demonstrates a further refinement and increase in
subtlety, due mostly to greater attention paid to the **formal** rather than
thematic aspects of Beckett's work. Although much of the first part of
her book contains the usual Beckett patter, Professor Cohn deserves

credit for signalling the concept (though I dislike her neologism) of 'theatereality' on the Beckettian stage, meaning that peculiar and jarring self-consciousness of Beckett characters which fuses theatre space and present reality. On Beckett's stage, the **real** world is only ever something remembered, something half-remembered, and much of his theatre exploits the ironic juxtaposition of such eminently non-realist events as an exploding parasol (in *Happy Days*) or burial up to the neck, with **representational fictions** fantasized by his characters. Having learned this much, Ruby Cohn still commits the blunder, however, of extracting representationalist significance from work that has taken so many pains to annihilate such optimistic notions. But all in all this tastes a lot less of American College Professor than I thought it would, earning *Just Play* just a place closer to the book on Beckett that has yet to be written. We might be waiting twenty years.

DG

THE WORLDS AND THE ACTIVISTS PAPERS by Edward Bond
(Eyre Methuen; £2.95 pb)

SPRING AWAKENING by Frank Wedekind translated by Edward Bond
(Eyre Methuen; £2.25 pb)

BOND: a study of his plays by Malcolm Hay and Philip Roberts
(Eyre Methuen; £3.95 pb)

Edward Bond seems to have struck a decidedly more dogmatic note of late, though the way the future's looking makes me wonder whether it isn't in fact the sanest and safest approach I've yet heard. His pronouncements on the rational and irrational ring out not only in his plays, but in the poems, the parables, and even in the introduction to his sharp translation of Wedekind's *Spring Awakening* used in the National Theatre production of 1974. It is a play now full of the angry talk of discontented adolescents—perhaps a language which Bond remembers first hand from sessions spent chewing the rag with young actors up and down the land.

Moritz: I don't belong here. Let them kick each other to bits. I'll shut the door
     behind me and walk away into freedom. Why should I let them push me about?

Elisabeth Bond has written an introductory life of Wedekind which examines his career and all his work in the context of an unready continent and a man forced into exile in several countries. In his own introduction Edward Bond ties the play to its modern relevance as a study of discipline and exploitation—teaching people that asking certain questions is wrong because it challenges their cosy vision of the status quo.

Wedekind remained one of Brecht's obsessions: Brecht remains one of Bond's. Indeed, he himself would probably not be too offended by the title Britain's Bitter Brecht. *The Activists Papers* (apart from containing many typographical errors) amounts to an anthology of Bond's recent thoughts and impressions while working *in* the theatre as opposed to *on* the theatre. They serve as an introduction—better might be as a postscript—to *The Worlds,* and 'need not be read in the order in which they are printed here.' No order, in fact, could remove an amount of repetition running through the pieces; like Brechtian parables they stand alone as testimonies to an impassioned faith in reason and the need for social change that have become Bond's watchwords. The at times painfully obscure casually rubs up against the brightly demonstrative:

The form of the new drama will be epic. The name is often misunderstood, partly because the form isn't yet fully developed. An epic play tells a story and says why it happened. This gives it a beginning, a middle and an end joined together in a truthful way. This isn't true of the theatre of the absurd. It sees life as meaningless: it has a beginning and an end but no middle. The bourgeois theatre is concerned only with anecdotes: they have a middle but no beginning and end.

And it is perhaps the pronouncements on theatre which had for me more interest than the cultural history Bond presents: interesting in that one sees at last the complex analyses the playwright has made before finding suitable voices for his own ideas: should there be a story? how central is character? how to convey feelings through the play's texture? Most of the suggested answers are here like mouthwatering sweets concealed in carefully chosen wrappers.

Hay and Roberts look like becoming the Fortnum and Mason of Bond's wares: sole purveyors of quality interpretations to the studious. You could almost imagine Bond being someone who shuns academic readings of his work deliberately because he fears this will alienate him from the large non-intellectual audience he wants to reach. Whether or not, he must have given considerable help to his two acolytes to produce a book which charts almost month by month a writer's agonizings with a muse in one ear and an urgent producer in another. His output to date of sixteen plays and one work for music by Hans Werner Henze (*Orpheus*) is also covered in enviable detail, and just as intriguing is a list of what Beckett would call 'trunk pieces'—definitely 'not available for performance, scrutiny or publication' says the note.

Doubtless the book will become required reading in Britain's places of learning—where, so I hear, Edward Bond is doing really quite well. Maybe one day our own commercial theatres will manage to catch up with the enthusiasm shown in Germany for our most underexposed serious writer.

Note: a review of *The Worlds* is printed in Gambit 36, together with an interview with Edward Bond.

DR

CREATING A ROLE
STANISLAVSKI'S LEGACY both by Constantin Stanislavski
(Eyre Methuen; both £3.95 pb)

'Every human being lives a factual, everyday life, but he can also live the life of his imagination.' This distinction between 'everyday life' and the imagination is the key to Stanislavski's conception of acting.

The actor begins his approach to a role by a reading of the play in which a miraculous, intuitive comprehension of certain elements of the play is hoped for, which must be retained at all costs. Subsequent analysis will build on these instinctive beginnings, 'through the conscious to the unconscious,' working over the various 'planes' of the text—external social, literary, aesthetic, psychological, physical, personal. In his description of these 'planes', the aesthetic—'with the sublayers of all that is theatrical, artistic'—consists in its analysis of visits to 'museums, picture galleries, old private homes.' Thence we proceed 'from the theatrical to the human,' giving life to the role by means of artistic imagination.

That the 'artistic' should occupy such menial and vital functions in the course of the same process is bemusing until we consider again the opening quotation. For Stanislavski the theatre occupies a separate domain—an illusion, literally occupying a few square feet of stage, the processes of which are self-sufficient. In other words, there is the world of 'everyday life' to which the theatre is a tiny, dispensable activity; and there is the world of imagination that expresses itself on the stage and to which 'everyday life' is somewhat banal.

Thus having defined the parameters of his theatre, Stanislavski consistently draws us toward the centre, both of text and performer:

> ... we go from the periphery to the centre, from the external, literal form of the play to its spiritual essence. [...] ... the process goes deeper, it goes down from the realm of the external, the intellectual, into that of the inner, the spiritual life.

The truth is 'buried' and must be dug out; but this is only possible (conceivable) within the confines of a stage—a rarefied world at whose heart lies spiritual truth, revealed by the imagination.

In the initial reading of a play, Stanislavski implies that a truth resides, awaiting discovery. There is no suggestion that a text can be made to say a myriad of things depending on one's approach, and that the creative responsibility is to be honest in directing how that statement may be interpreted. In short, he restricts the link between the stage (the imagination) and the audience ('everyday life'). It is important to 'believe in what I am doing' as a character on stage, but not as a member of society on stage. Thus the intellect is distinguished from the imagination, rather than being intrinsically bound, and fulfils a peripheral, 'external' function.

Creating a Role offers a recapitulation of ideas expressed in *Building a Character* and *An Actor Prepares,* in the form of particular workings of 'Woe From Wit' and 'Othello'. Its usefulness is its particularity in this respect—a kind of 'Stanislavski at Work'.

Stanislavski's Legacy is in some ways the more revealing work. Its fragmentary form complements the usually more systematic style of his writings and juxtaposes casual insights into a variety of subjects. For instance, Stanislavski describes his theatre as 'thoughtful, high-minded, popular' and agreed with Tolstoy's assertion that 'the theatre is the most powerful pulpit of our times'. However, he also writes: 'the most valuable things in our art can only be communicated by the means of the creative emotions of the individual actor,' and elsewhere of a 'contagious, mass emotion' in which 'the spectators hypnotize each other.' This emotional link is clearly how Stanislavski envisaged education in the theatre. 'The best way to be in contact with the audience is to be in close relationship with characters in the play.'

> People come into the theatre for entertainment, but without their being aware of it, they leave it with awakened emotions and thoughts, enriched by the experience of having witnessed the beautiful life of a human spirit.
> The components of your excitement are such that they force you to concentrate to turn your eye inward . . . you sit around the samovar and talk intimately about the problems of life, one's philosophic outlook, social problems . . . the effect on your eyes and ears is only a means to penetrate the soul of an audience.

But what is to be imparted to an audience? An actor is 'a teacher of beauty and truth.' A playwright is 'bound to reveal the soul of his people, the details of their life, the things that affect their psychology.'

But here the process stops. Beyond discussion there is no prescription for action on the part of the audience. For all his social concern, Stanislavski makes no direct link between acting and political action; not so much that this would demean the function of theatre, as that the theatre is conceived as a separate place where truth is merely displayed rather than being at work in the 'outside world': 'The revolution will come from something inside. We shall see on stage the metamorphosis of the soul of the world, the inner struggle with a worn-out past.'

Ultimately, Stanislavski's writings convey a man who, surrounded by a corrupt and ossified society, saw theatre as 'something to bring light and beauty into our humdrum lives,' profoundly pessimistic of the notion that light and beauty could become our lives. Hence the view which the playwright himself constantly rejected—that Chekhov's plays were tragedies rather than comedies or even farces. Indeed, such pessimism is inherent in a theatre that presumes to demonstrate social structure without taking the necessary steps to demonstrate its mutability; without such detachment, laughter can quickly turn to tears, and yet without the truth that Stanislavski demanded, social structure is not demonstrated in its finer detail, and the quality of mutability is falsified.

The double standard that Stanislavski espoused with regard to the

metamorphosis expected of an actor compared to the relative stasis of
a member of the audience or even a character in a play, is well
demonstrated by contrasting a text by Tolstoy, which Stanislavski quotes
in support of his argument and his views on, respectively, the personality
of an actor and his role.

> People are like rivers: they all contain the same water everywhere, yet each
> river at times will be narrow, swift, broad, smooth-flowing, clear, cold, muddy,
> warm. So it is with people. Each man carries within himself the germs of all
> human qualities.
>
> (Leo Tolstoy)

Stanislavski uses this observation to support his argument against type-casting
of actors: 'to transform oneself physically and spiritually is the first and
principal object of acting art.' Yet in the same fragment he writes, 'there
is no person on earth who does not possess his own individual character.
Even the most colourless person is distinguished by his character of utter
lack of colour.'

Transformation as described by Tolstoy is, in the context of Stanislavski's
naturalism, the preserve of the actor. The audience is encouraged to discuss
transformation 'around the samovar'; it is enabled to witness it on stage,
and in Chekhov's case to infer it in society; but the possibility to experience
it is necessarily restricted by the structure of the event. Stanislavski
introduced imagination to modern acting; it yet remains to be instilled in
the audience, let alone 'everyday life'.

M. Binns

THE ENTERTAINERS by Clive Unger-Hamilton (ed.)

(Pitman; £9.95 cb)

'For early man a *play* was a serious matter.'
'Samuel Beckett made nihilism popular.'
Thus *The Entertainers,* a chronological Who Was/Who Is Who aimed at
those who haven't yet pawned their coffee-table. Edward Bond emerges
as a kind of stage-struck psychopath, but on the whole the entries are
what you would expect in two-hundred words from an AA guide book.
In its favour, it is colourful and reasonably comprehensive. Could *you*
speak for three minutes on Giovan Battista Della Porta . . . or Alexander
Herrmann . . . or Hiram W. Davis . . . or Tom Stoppard . . . GONG!

Circus freaks, puppeteers, cabaret, mime, opera and kabuki all find a
place. But to quote Sylvester Schultz Jnr., 'what you learn from this,
you will never have needed to know.'

MB

FROM FRINGE TO FLYING CIRCUS: Celebrating a Unique Generation of Comedy 1960–80 by Roger Wilmut

(Eyre Methuen; £7.95 cb)

After *Beyond the Fringe,* the 'Oxbridge Mafia' moved substantially into television, and as John Bird points out, 'originality of material and approach . . . is an anathema to television.' Whatever bite the satire of *TWTWTW* and *Not So Much A Programme* may have had was killed off effectively enough for *Not the Nine O'Clock News,* fifteen years later, to seem entirely fresh and daring. However, for the most part, the bite was never meant to be that bloody. Alan Bennett recalls: 'We were having it both ways. Most of the stuff was in the tradition of English revue—light, silly, very funny.' Miller: 'I wasn't angry or annoyed, I was slightly "nettled".' Rushton's impersonations of MacMillan were apparently enjoyed by the then Prime Minister, one of the first of the long line of Cabinet Jesters (Rushton, I mean; or perhaps not). By the time of *Monty Python,* by way of Pete and Dud and *I'm Sorry I'll Read That Again,* there had ceased to be any specific 'targets' at all; merely virtuoso absurdity that was all the more compulsive for coming to us by courtesy of the stuffiest of institutions.

Such aimless humour, however bright and spontaneous, is bound eventually to pall. (Incidentally, I disagree with Mr Wilmut's assertion that *Python* killed off the 'beginning-middle-end' sketch, apart from in *The Two Ronnies.* What about Morecambe and Wise, the Tommy Cooper and Mike Yarwood shows? It, and 'situation comedy' are still safe and predominant modes.) In a sense this has been the weakness of all the Oxbridge comedy from *Fringe* onwards: its penetration was only skin-deep. Its strength was in command and richness of language, but the use to which this was put was largely a 'comedy of manners'. It was drawing-room stuff, which is, I suppose, where most televisions are to be found. What satire there was concerned personalities; the language of even working-class characters was filtered through middle-class dictionaries (Pete and Dud's tramps); *Python's* anarchy was of a reassuring kind.

This was partly a result of the medium and its controllers; mostly it was due to the background and aims of the protagonists. It took an American cabaret comic—Lenny Bruce—to lay bare the twin bastions of society: sex and money. 'Bruce was a bloodbath where *Beyond the Fringe* had been a pinprick' (Ken Tynan). It took a working-class playwright— Joe Orton—to make real use of the mastery of language that distinguished most of the humour of this period. By contrast, Bennett, Cook, Bron, Bird Jones, Cleese et al. appear coy and almost wasted.

That said, they can be very, very funny, and the pity of Mr Wilmut's rather dry book is that more room is not found for the scripts themselves, since the detailed historical commentary he adds often seems less than rivetingly significant. Worse still, the design of the book—with tiny black and white illustrations like bacteria slides—loses an opportunity for what is, at the very least, a highly colourful subject.

MB

PUNCH AT THE THEATRE by Sheridan Morley (ed.)
(Robson Books; £6.50 cb; 192pp)

Punch boasts a long and intimate liaison with the theatre, dating back to its birth in 1841—the name itself being derived from Punch and Judy (hence also 'punch' line?). Sheridan Morley's connection—if not as long—is at least as intimate, even as regards onomastics, I suspect. His anthology of the magazine's century-and-a-half of humorous pieces, articles, and of course those inimitable cartoons, surpasses mere corporate narcissism, however, and even non-afficionados such as myself might find dipping into it in the taxi on the way to an opening a sure remedy for press-night dread.

The pre-World War II eras are more copiously represented by cartoons rather than prose, which I find a good balance, whereas the second half of the 20th century reverses editorial priorities, which is not to say that the work of Robert Searle and that master theatre caricaturist William Hewison are not given ample space. There are some very funny and sometimes hilarious pieces by Alan Coren (Lord Olivier's maiden speech in the House Of Lords, as well as an Aussie rendition of the Oedipus myth, 'Oedipus Bruce'), among others, while Morley's own version of *The Caretaker* as directed by Noël Coward is a charming blend of wit and pastiche. Striking a more serious chord now and then, original reviews by *Punch* critics pop up amid the fun-poking. Most readable of these I think is Eric Keown's slating of *Look Back in Anger* in its first production at the Royal Court. But most of all I enjoyed the section on Amateur Dramatics, so easy to make fun of, but done here so well.

DG

THE THEATRE EVENT: Modern Theories of Performance by Timothy J. Wiles
(Univ. of Chicago; £10.50 cb)

In the convoluted prose that seems to distinguish a certain kind of American academic, Timothy Wiles attempts to analyze Stanislavski, Brecht and Artaud in terms of their own personal interpretations of catharsis, which, he claims, may bear little resemblance to Aristotle's original meaning. He, however, does not venture to suggest his own interpretation. The result is a twisting of the words of these thinkers into a maze of paraphrasing for no particularly cogent reason; so twisted in fact that we arrive in the chapter on Brecht at what is supposed to be a theory of the 'schizoid actor'. Such literature may help fill draughty gaps on university bookshelves, but I fail to see what it has to do with theatre, except to mystify. Far better to consult the authors themselves.

MB

THE DRAMATIC CRITICISM OF ALEXANDER WOOLLCOTT
by Morris U. Burns

(Scarecrow Press; $15.00 cb)

Woollcott was drama critic on the New York Times and Herald between the wars. His reflections ramble like half-awake chat in the New England home of a Henry James novel. They are affectionate, ignorant and impressionistic, with all the penetration of a stage dagger. Yet they reek of sincerity, particularly in his occasional, mild attacks on censorship. As an indicator of the American theatre before O'Neill and Williams, they reflect precisely its rather lost, 'colonial' character: the lull before the melodrama. Layout and design of the book are dreary, broken-up into very short fragments with too many comments interspersed by the editor, and about half is taken up with a presumably 'definitive' index of Woollcott's articles.

MB

REQUIEM by Francis Warner

(Colin Smythe; £3.25 pb)

CHESS IN THE MIRROR: a study of theatrical cubism in Francis Warner's *Requiem* and its *Maquettes* by Rosalind Jeffrey

(J. Thornton; £5.00 cb)

The name of Samuel Beckett crops up in these works as a dedication (among the plays) and as an antecedent (in the introduction and Ms Jeffrey's criticism), but Warner's language is more reminiscent of the later Eliot— minus a bit of prudery—in its aridity, biblical allusiveness and tone, and in its portentous stuffiness.

> Old man: It's a temporal world. Always becoming its own past tense.
> *(Troat)*

As in Eliot, the self-conscious poesy creates a tangential effect in the characters that removes all sense of tension or reality . . . and thus of drama. The observations are hackneyed:

> Actress: We know so much!
> Actor: *(correcting her)*: Enough to know a little.
> *(Lumen)*

The humour, or what I presume is intended as humour, is often painful.

> Bride Two: It was morning.
> Bride One: Mourning? At our wedding?
> *(Emblem)*

Which brings us to the disturbing frequency with which sex is associated with death.

Gonad *(sardonic)*: Let me kiss your open grave.

Or again:

Gonad: The price of love is death.

(Lying Figures)

Such puritanism is obscene.

Rosalind Jeffrey's criticism of Warner's six plays tries to establish from them a Theatre of Cubism. Cubism was an attack by visual artists, working in two dimensions, on the spatial restrictions of perspective. Theatre is three-dimensional and it is only an academic concoction to regard a sequence of verbal images as 'cubist'. Furthermore, Ms Jeffrey seems to admire those qualities I fault, so those who find significance in Mr Warner's work may find riches here.

MB

IBSEN AND THE THEATRE by Errol Durbach (ed)
(Macmillan; £15 cb)

This book is a collection of eight papers delivered at the 'Ibsen and the Theatre' conference, sponsored by the University of British Columbia in Vancouver in May 1978 to celebrate the 150th anniversary of Henrik Ibsen's birth. They contain very little new or original research on Ibsen or his plays. Nevertheless, taken as a whole they manage to provide a commendable introduction to the man and his work. Commendable in that, although imbued with great enthusiasm for their subject, they are alive to the fact that Ibsen has always aroused controversy, in his subject matter, his staging, his language, his concern with 'ordinary' people, and his (for his time) revolutionary abandomnent of the artificialities of plot, which in turn demanded a fresh approach to the acting. Joyce's youthful admiration of Ibsen is often quoted but it is worth remembering that what the 19-year-old undergraduate at University College, Dublin, most admired was the Norwegian playwright's inner exile: 'your lofty impersonal power . . . how in your indifference to public canons of art, friends and shibboleths you walked in the light of your inward heroism.'

Michael Meyer's chapter provides a brief but interesting resumé of the dramatist's life, and this together with the bibliography accumulated from the notes to each essay supplies ample material to orientate any would-be student of Ibsen. The variety of perspectives in the book also conveys the need to approach the study of theatre from many sides, to recognize the full complexities of a text and a production of that text. In his introduction to the essays Errol Durbach records one of their major lessons when he writes, 'in confronting us with the reality of poetic loss in English translation, they also alert us to the essentially provisional nature of the judgments we, as non-Norwegian readers, make on Ibsen's texts.' Equally, the fourth chapter of the book offers a brief stage history of Ibsen's plays, showing the essentially provisional nature of any mise-en-scène, and thus proclaiming the need for each new generation to continually re-stage and re-interpret 'classic' texts.

Evert Sprinchorn in his contribution highlights the tendency in past productions of Ibsen to underestimate the importance of some of the secondary characters thus allowing their portrayal to degenerate into stereotype or caricature: the dramatic stature of Nora, in *The Doll's House*, and Hedda in *Hedda Gabler* is diminished if their husbands are played as mere foils for the leading ladies, and yet this has been the custom when casting these plays. Sprinchorn calls for a re-appraisal of these secondary roles in order to emphasize the energy they contribute to the complex network of relationships which give the plays their true dynamic. In the fifth chapter, Martin Esslin sees Ibsen as responsible for the introduction in theatre of what he calls the 'principle of uncertainty' whereby the drama does not unfold directly and predictably but rather through a more subtle, often oblique use of dialogue is gradually brought to a dénouement which is more a discovery than a logical conclusion. And in this invention of the 'principle of uncertainty' Esslin denotes the birth of modern absurdist drama, the static, non-communicating pieces of Beckett and Pinter, the *no-man's land* of the modern stage. Janet Suzman gives an account of how she approached the role of Hedda Gabler and offers some insight on the manner in which an experienced actress can enhance her performance by thinking through the part.

A useful, stimulating little book, then, but at £15 for a mere 144 pages, best consulted in the library.

John Lyons

SHAKESPEARE'S IMAGES OF PREGNANCY by Elizabeth Sacks
(Macmillan; £12.00 cb)

The term 'conception' suggests both childbirth and thought. Elizabeth Sacks records the growing use of this *double entendre* from the mid-sixteenth century and throughout Shakespeare's work. Unfortunately, it is not in itself a particularly pregnant idea. There is something of a confusion between the use of the childbearing image as a metaphor for thought and as a theme in itself, and it is not always clear whether Ms Sacks is concerned with the creativity of thought or the 'image of pregnancy' as a metaphor. In fact, the metaphor is so mixed with the literal that we do not learn an awful lot from this work, which largely amounts to a (not very comprehensive) catalogue of Shakespeare's bawdy puns, romantic fantasies and remarks upon the fruitfulness of man and nature. Neither was I convinced by the notion that the use of sexual imagery to describe mental creativity could be in any way a form of male 'womb-envy' corresponding to the female 'penis-envy'. Are we to construe from this that women would not have perceived the creative aspects of thought as analogous to reproduction?   MB

ALL ON STAGE: CHARLES WYNDHAM AND THE ALBERYS
by Wendy Trewin

(Harrap; £9.95 cb)

Wyndham's and Albery's. 'How many of the thousands who know these theatres in today's West End of London ever give a thought to Wyndham or Albery?' asks Wendy Trewin. If you are one who has, then this solidly researched account of Victorian and Edwardian middle-class theatre, using the Wyndham family archives, should provide fuel for several more. Unfortunately, this has to be one of the least satisfying periods of English theatre history: the age of the actor-manager who took so wearily long to dislodge. However, an excellently prepared and illustrated account for all that, and one that it would otherwise be hard to fault.

MB

LEARNING THROUGH THEATRE: Essays and Casebooks on Theatre in Education by Tony Jackson (ed)
(Manchester University Press; £5.50 pb)

'The role of T.I.E. is a distinct one,' Gordon Vallins tells us in the introduction to *Learning Through Theatre,* and in the course of the book this role emerges, basically, as teaching with the aid of theatrical techniques. Its origins lie within the theatre rather than the education system (as do the origins of most of its exponents) and it is perhaps for this very reason that T.I.E. faces its greatest problem, aside from sheer finance: acceptability within the education system. Vallins himself draws attention to 'the lack of any evidence of schools making positive use of T.I.E. as part of the general rethinking of their role and their curriculum' and to the fact that 'resistance to the notion of theatre as a teaching instrument [. . .] seems deeply ingrained in institutional attitudes.'

All the contributors argue for a deeper involvement of T.I.E. companies with teachers and school administrators, but the fundamental problem lies in the nature of the education system itself and its ability to assimilate more imaginative approaches. In this respect T.I.E. can be a 'necessary "gingerer" in the system' as Tony Jackson suggests; or as David Pammenter puts it, 'counter-balance the pressures and demands of an institutionalized system of education' which 'reinforces the class structure that created it.'

Thus, one is hopeful that T.I.E. can be a genuine innovator and may achieve more than 'the stimulus-potential, designed to enhance the curriculum,' with which Kathy Joyce seems content. It is the whole field of 'play in learning' that is under-developed, certainly at secondary school level, while the necessity—frequently mentioned here—for T.I.E. to work with small classes, is not its alone, but possibly the largest problem in education at the moment.

The specific value of T.I.E., as expressed in the *Poverty Knocks* casebook, is that the children are placed in unaccustomed positions of responsibility 'with a considerable range of identities experienced by each child;' or, as Gavin Bolton puts it, 'a highly structured living-through experience.' By and large, the children in question are involved in experiencing situations and responsibilities to an extent the 'adult' theatre might well envy.

Whereas the eleven essays that form the first two-thirds of the book are theoretical introductions to various, sometimes overlapping, aspects of T.I.E., the three casebooks that follow provide the more immediate, practical account and are interesting in that they seem to indicate a declining use of physical participation and an increasing use of performance (followed by discussion) as the audience age increases. The programme for infants—*It Fits*—takes as its subject thought-process itself, incorporating De Bono's concept of lateral thinking and demonstrating that 'T.I.E. can deal with subjects other than English, Drama, History and Social Studies. *It Fits* did manage to open up fresh ways of looking at and grasping mathematical concepts.' The two casebooks for older children are of a more political nature and indeed it seems largely agreed among the contributors that the role of T.I.E. lies predominantly in promoting social and ethical awareness.

Interesting too that Pam Schweitzer considers a situation in which children are unaware of the artificial nature of the conditions—*Ifan's Valley*— and consequently live through the process of decision-making, to be a 'Theatre of Reality'. Surely, it is the theatre of illusion and depends on the naivety of the pupils for its success. To this extent the actor-teacher occupies a specific function in that his words will be mistaken for reality, and offers as Bernard Crick suggests, 'at best a good substitute for an encounter with the person being played.' In the case of *Ifan's Valley*, the device is employed to good effect, but it is important to remember that such 'cons' can be and are daily used to the contrary.

In a sense, Pam Schweitzer makes the same mistake as Brian Wilks in seeing theatre as illusion, whereas it is essentially language. While sympathizing with Wilks in his wish to avoid 'an insipid, orthodox and safe method in educational drama which could be easily accommodated within the existing school structures,' it is precisely his fears of 'sociological urban guerillas' with 'a bias that elsewhere would provide waves of anger' that are of a type likely to create it. For the idea that theatre is an illusion, that it can reflect 'real life', perpetuates the myth that impartiality is a possibility beyond the parameters of a sport or game.

T.I.E. fulfils a specific role. However, it is to be wished that such imaginative, intimate, child-centred education techniques develop in all subjects and that theatre's particular contribution of role-playing can develop more amorphously in the whole field of education.

MB

ALFRED JARRY: NIHILISM AND THE THEATER OF THE ABSURD
by Maurice Marc LaBelle

(New York U.P. £4.75 pb)

SELECTED WORKS OF ALFRED JARRY edited by Roger Shattuck and Simon Watson Taylor

(Eyre Methuen £3.95 pb)

Dada, Surrealism, Theatre of Cruelty, Theatre of the Absurd: Alfred Jarry, legend tells us, was grandfather or guru to them all. He is widely revered as the author of one earth-shaking play, *Ubu Roi,* first performed in 1896 and recently on view in French at the Young Vic, in Milliganese at the Jeanetta Cochrane, and, infinitely repeatable, in Cyril Connolly's masterly version on the Open University screen. The purpose of Maurice LaBelle's book is to remind us that there is more in Jarry's work than the hideously memorable saga of Pa Ubu. Only in the last few pages is Jarry's posthumous influence considered, and this 'first comprehensive study of Jarry in English' presents instead a roughly chronological account of Jarry's life and works: juvenilia, dramatic theory and sources, the Ubu cycle, and fiction *post Ubum,* a subject not promised by the book's sub-title. Nor are we to be entertained with the absorbing trivia of Jarry's earthly existence: the legendary capacity for alcohol, the macabre practical jokes, the amazing feats of marksmanship practised on spiders, apple trees, café mirrors. Maurice LaBelle wishes to detach Jarry the artist from the self-created legend, and to expose the 'affectionate and very sentimental' man who took refuge behind the speech and gestures of his monstrous puppet. Thus we are given succinct, studious accounts of all Jarry's more or less important writings, samples designed presumably to whet our appetite for the originals.

But this may not be the effect. Much has been written on Jarry in recent years, in French and English (is it too soon to speak of an Ubindustry?); Maurice LaBelle has read it all and is generous with citation and bibliography. However, he has reacted against his predecessors' sometimes uncritical admiration for most of Jarry's works, and his own analysis of each piece, following his summary, often shows a disturbing lack of sympathy with his subject. Long ago, Jacques Lemarchand advised early patrons of Ionesco to leave outside their inherited theatrical prejudices, the 'Spartan fox' gnawing away beneath their stuffed shirts; Maurice LaBelle's fox sinks its fangs deep, causing him to denounce Jarry for illogicality, superficiality, incapacity for sustained analysis, and especially lack of precision; he quotes, but does not heed, Jarry's dictum that 'to describe is to lose three quarters of the pleasure of the poem'; one might add that to explain all for the benefit of the 'average spectator' is to lose the rest. He deplores Jarry's ignorance of economics and politics, precisely what saved Jarry from lining up with many of the prize bores of his era. Paradoxically, LaBelle's analysis of *Ubu Roi* highlights its social satire and underplays the formal innovations, particularly the endless theatrical parody which is the play's most original feature. We are constantly told what Jarry could and should have done with his material, had he but observed traditional academic norms. Jarry is constantly refused licence to play, like his great mentor Rabelais (unjustly removed in this book from the pedestal to which Jarry hoisted him). Praise and blame are distributed on a descending scale from 'effective' to 'sophomoric': indeed, throughout the book, we seem to see Professor LaBelle grading second-year essays— and Jarry, A.H., rarely rises above gamma plus.

For those who wish to judge for themselves, it is a pleasure to welcome the paperback reissue of *Selected Works of Alfred Jarry,* first published in 1965. The book is not devoted exclusively to the theatre, and contains neither of the full-length Ubu plays, which are easily available elsewhere. On the other hand, it includes all Jarry's substantial essays on the theatre, centring round his presentation of *Ubu Roi,* as well as another sparkling Connolly translation, of the slighter *Ubu cocu.* The selection of poetry, essays and fiction includes the whole of Jarry's Rabelaisian (in the literary sense) masterpiece *Dr Faustroll,* usefully annotated by Simon Watson Taylor, and Roger Shattuck's sympathetic introduction deftly orientates the reader in the bizarre world of the Great Iconoclast.

Michael Heath

OTHER SPACES by Colin Chambers

(Methuen Theatrefile; £2.25 pb)

Colin Chambers has astutely plotted the development of The Royal Shakespeare Company's two 'studio' theatres (a vogue that hit several of our larger companies during the Seventies)—the Other Place in Stratford and the Warehouse in London. It is a fresh, passionate account that pays full tribute to the important foundation laid by Buzz Goodbody as well as tracing the early experiments in small scale productions at other venues.

A wealth of detailed information, well researched and presented, covers the plays, writers, directors and locations, as well as the effect that this important attention to a closer, smaller production has had on theatrical output. The list can only be called impressive when one considers the classic productions, new work, and the revival of recent work (Bond, Brenton, Wood). The result is a highly valuable book, a necessity for anyone who touches the theatre . . . and a work to be returned to many times in the future.

R. James

CORIOLANUS IN EUROPE by David Daniell

(Athlone Press: £9.95 cb)

In 1979 the Royal Shakespeare Company toured Europe with Terry Hands' production of *Coriolanus*. Mr. Daniell, an English lecturer, accompanied them on the eight city Shakespearian stop-over, keeping a journal of the trip. This has been expanded to include insights into the play, particularly the political point of view (what it could mean to modern Europe) and the interpretation of characters (after conversations with the players themselves). He quotes at times straight from the journal: 'I take my paranoia for a walk, having disguised it from myself for long enough,' mixing these rather unnecessary personal remarks with observations on the play . . . especially Brecht's version and the description of the Company itself.

The team of stagehands, actors and musicians faced a plethora of problems in each city, starting with stage facilities and ending with audience reaction. The final product is a book confused in parts as to what were its real intentions. However, there are passages helpful to an understanding of the play's difficulties, showing the barriers with which the Company was faced in its production, rather than just a scholarly reading that a purely critical approach would employ. A book liberally illustrated with location snapshots and Company photographs.

RJ

ENGLISH NATIONAL OPERA GUIDES: 1–4
La Cenerentola, Aida, The Magic Flute, Fidelio
(John Calder; £2.00 each; pb)

This is a good start to what promises to be a very useful and reasonably priced series of opera handbooks. For the price of a budget record one gets three articles by different writers on various aspects of the operas, a libretto in the original language with a full English version, a thematic guide, a discography and a bibliography. Most of the articles are newly commissioned and it is in these new articles that I found greatest pleasure, particularly Philip Gosset's 'Fairy Tale and Opera Buffa' in *La Cenerentola* and Rodney Milnes' 'Singspiel and Symbolism' in *The Magic Flute*. One especially rewarding inclusion is 'Cinderella in Performance', two discussions with the conductor Mark Elder and the producer Colin Graham. The light this throws on the opera is of great value both to the newcomer as to the seasoned opera-goer. I hope future guides will make more of the interviews to give a more informal and varied presentation to the series. Not all the articles are new; there is, for instance, an extract from Romain Rolland's study 'Beethoven the Creator', first published in 1928 and currently out of print.

Opera guides such as these fall between the serious monograph on Verdi or Wagner and the ENO/Covent Garden Opera Programme. This is not a criticism of the series, but pinpoints its strength. The serious monograph is not likely to be read by the average opera-goer, and by the time one buys a programme in the opera house there is little time to savour the erudition and insights offered. These guides will, I hope, tempt some people to read about the opera and know the libretto before the performance.

Opera is going to have to fight harder to justify its lion's share of the Arts Council subsidy in the future. The only hope for a more financially secure future lies not in increased sponsorship (even these guides have The Stock Exchange and The National Westminster Bank to thank for sponsoring two issues in the series) but in the education of a larger public to the appreciation of a larger range of operas. One way ENO is doing this is by introducing masterpieces from all ages side by side with less well-known works such as Prokofiev's *War and Peace,* Weber's *Euryanthe* and Gounod's *Romeo and Juliet,* let alone their crusading for Janáček and Massenet. The other way for the enterprising spirit to flourish hopefully lies in this bright new collaboration with Calder books.

Timothy Coombs

THE ROMANS IN BRITAIN by Howard Brenton
(Eyre Methuen; £2.50 pb)

What is there to be said about *The Romans in Britain* that hasn't been said—or at any rate imagined? Correspondence in the Guardian spanned almost four weeks, and as I write, the thwarted Mary Whitehouse is seeking to prosecute the director for the procuring of men for indecent acts! It is unfortunate that the sensationalism surrounding the production of Brenton's most recent epic play has overshadowed the writing itself. His acute verbal power and fine description is not all lost in this work, yet ultimately the subject suffers. The concern is familiar Brenton territory—domination (both individual and imperial) and his displeasure at the British state.

This analysis of foreign occupation is set in three ages: the Roman invasion of 54BC, Britian in 515AD and Ireland in 1980. The most successful writing occurs in the modern scenes where a British Army officer is hiding in a cornfield. Edges and information are very blurred and inconclusive, which helps neither the dramatic power, nor the author's intention. The language and plot in 54BC are insubstantial and wander, coming to a close when Caesar returns as a modern day army officer. *Romans in Britian* lacks the cohesion and tightness of *Weapons of Happiness,* as well as that work's ability to paint a wide canvas of historical background, and really only lights up with the unexpected ending when the Arthurian legend is conjured up.

RJ

MEDIATIONS: Brecht, Beckett and the Media by Martin Esslin
(Eyre Methuen; £8.95 cb)

In 'The Icon and the Self-Portrait', one of the three essays on Brecht in this book, Esslin comes close to, but finally just misses, the most important feature of Brecht's Marxism. He describes it at one point as providing a 'discipline' and a 'tradition' and at another as supplying for Brecht 'the foundations of a truly scientific aesthetics of drama'. He then goes on to characterize that discipline as a 'restraint for his wild, inspirational outbursts' and to reduce that 'scientific aesthetics' to mere pragmatic observation after the event. By this barely perceptible shift from analysis to personal interpretation he transforms what for Brecht was a *method* (present-day sceptics would in any case baulk at invoking science here, especially to translate *Wissenschaft*) into an *object* (in this case, presumably a strait-jacket), and thereby reduces what is essentially a philosophical approach with its own historical background, social purpose and practical application, to an immutable declaration of faith which can be judged right or wrong by a schoolmasterly tick. He allows his own critical function to become a head hand on a living critical process which for Brecht was the source of a new creative initiative.

This is not a new attitude to Brecht's Marxism for Esslin—it was well enough expressed in *A Choice of Evils*. The sad thing is that the 'enormous volume of useless, time-wasting and intellectually destructive scholasticism' (his view of the material that has followed his own publication) hasn't produced even a flicker of doubt in his own unbending certainty. However much one may incline to agree with Esslin in his broad response to that 'scholasticism', its principal benefit has been its emphasis on dialectical method, the relating of subjective to social, the attempt to see a historical context in which the one can even produce the other. It is a discipline which requires keeping both in mind, living with their frequently contradictory relationship, and regarding 'truth' as relative to both, not removed to the neutral, frozen plane of abstract imagery as in Beckett (to whom he devotes six essays).

One does not need to know that Esslin, as he describes himself—borrowing from Brecht—has 'changed his countries oftener than his shoes' to share his horror of Stalinist oppression. Yet his resistance to left-wing analysis amounts at times to the same wilful self-delusion he accuses Brecht of. Does he seriously imagine that a man who took pains to get an Austrian passport before living in East Berlin could write a series of songs (the *Herrnburger Bericht*) condemning the West German authorities for blocking free movement between the two Germanies without anticipating its effect on the East German authorities? Was it not more likely to have been an implicit challenge? Surely if Esslin believes that the man who commented on the arrest of old Communists in the Soviet Union by saying 'The more innocent they are, the more they deserve to die' was in fact advocating resistance to Stalin, he can't have written the *Herrnburger Bericht*, as Esslin claims, in 'innocence and naiveté.'

No, Brecht saw very clearly the barbarism of Russian soldiers occupying Berlin, the provincialism of East Berlin's ruling elite, the vestiges of Nazism in local officials. But the question for him was whether 'existing Socialism' (to borrow from Bahro) would deal with these questions as well as the material ones. Twice in this book Esslin refers to Brecht's deliberations on the gap between socialist aspiration and its daily operation as 'touching' in its naiveté—an inappropriate put-down if ever there was one. For where does the real naiveté lie? In the essay 'Brecht in Chinese Garb' he quotes a passage from the excellent *Book of Twists and Turns,* assuming it to be an example of Brecht forcing himself to be enthusiastic about those responsible for sending people to labour camps. In fact he completely misinterprets the ironic force of this description of the bureaucrats responsible: 'They are condemned to improve the social institutions of the country. Those against whom a law case used to be necessary are turned into people conducting a law case.'

However great Esslin's own naiveté in dealing with Brecht's 'twists and turns', his distaste for the frequent and loose bandying of the term 'Brechtian' is laudable, as is his final point that amongst the great mass of recent scholarship there has been no convincing work to establish whether the A-effect actually does what it's supposed to. And it is in this more pragmatic vein, in his essays on Reinhardt ('Creator of the Modern German Theatre'), on 'Beckett and the Art of Broadcasting' and on radio drama ('The Mind as a Stage') that he is at his best. Largely descriptive accounts of practical work, these essays afford major insights into the various praxes they recount and have the solidity of experience rather than propagandistic speculation behind them.

When he gets on to discussing television as a mass medium however, his worthwhile practical observations mix increasingly with social assumptions similar to those underlying his approach to Brecht, and his argument begins to unravel. On the one hand it is wonderful to see him observe firmly that the availability of more channels in a commercially operated system seems to restrict rather than increase the choice for the viewer; also to see the recognition—in contrast to the usual glib assumption that the sheer volume and blandness of the TV diet dulls people's critical faculties—that it produces 'a highly critical and sophisticated [. . .] community hardened and immunised against both the overt and the hidden manipulators.'

On the other hand his description of 'folk art' as 'crude, vulgar, repetitive, unoriginal, poorly characterised and sentimental' possibly tells us more about Esslin than the thing he purports to describe. 'The mass media,' he cries, '*alas*, are and will remain media for the masses.' (My italics.) Ah, of course, Them.

In 'Aristotle and the Advertisers', a wildly flown kite equating TV ads with primitive ritual drama, he claims: 'There is a vast unexpressed, subconscious yearning *in these people*, not only for the consumer goods concerned, but also for the hidden forces and the miraculous action of the spirits inhabiting them.' (My italics.) And meanwhile, I wonder, what are those other people, the intellectual middle class, who are presumably not included, yearning for? Or is he saying, like sweating and picking your nose, that 'yearning' is something they don't do? To my mind the qualities he lists (borrowing from Boeckelmann): 'personalisation of the subject matter, concentration on success and achievement, novelty, stress on the advantages of normality, the appeal of wealth,' etc., characterise that class just as accurately, if not more so, than 'the masses'. If one is looking for the emotional pressure-points which make TV so effective, one is better off looking into these areas rather than 'yearning', as Esslin seems to, for 'arguments above a certain level of abstraction'.

He is closer to the mark, for example, when he points to repetition, rhyme and rhythm as being what makes commercials stick in the memory, than he is when assuming that 'the vast majority of mankind . . . remains on a fairly primitive level of intellectual development.' He is certainly wrong to presume that a large number of schoolteachers are not at pains to develop in their pupils a critical alertness to the manipulations of the media. But above all he would be far better off questioning the value of the bloodless 'ability to think abstractly' than beginning to talk of 'genetic limitations' (sic).

We are all, to a greater or lesser extent, susceptible to the various emotional and intellectual manipulations the box is capable of, and thank goodness a profoundly alienated critical suspicion exists in both East and West to resist it. But having claimed the advantage of state-controlled media over those controlled by market forces alone, he then assumes that only the states of the evil East will be looking to serve their own interests: 'In a society with a free press, for example, the competition amongst newspapers alone will ensure that there can be no question of topics for discussion being chosen by a small clique of manipulators.' Does he seriously imagine that a press which is entirely privately-owned is any less prone to trivialization and bias than a national TV service under the same circumstances? Or does he rest assured that '*more* rather than less manipulation would be needed to improve it' (his italics), provided that manipulation is in the Western hands–'genetic limitations' and all–of which he approves, rather than the Eastern ones of which he doesn't?

The truth of the matter is that neither in the East nor the West do the media actually belong to the mass. Instead we have bigger or smaller self-perpetuating cliques of pundits assuming what the masses want, speculating as to how they think, and, time and time again, getting it palpably wrong.

Steve Gooch

STAGES IN THE REVOLUTION: Political Theatre in Britain Since 1968 by Catherine Itzin

(Eyre Methuen; £4.50pb)

'All theatre is political. But the significant theatre of 1968-78 was primarily theatre of political change.' Thus, Cathy Itzin defines the subject of her book, but from within the compass of that definition emerge two broadly different approaches to the business of both reflecting and influencing that change. On the one hand, a theatre that works with audiences on their own territory—the community hall, the shop floor, the pub or club—often creating a new audience and venues; on the other hand, the approach of 'strategic penetration' into the established theatre or television network. By and large, authors and companies have chosen to work predominantly in one or other of these areas. The value of Itzin's book is that, by considering the exponents of these two areas together in the one volume, and in allowing them to speak for themselves, she highlights the essential unity of aim within political theatre, even though this unity is not always recognized by the writers or groups involved. The same questions and criticisms tend to arise: Is community theatre or agit-prop theatre effective? Is it superficial, offering easy answers for stereotype situations and characters? Is working in the established networks a sell-out? Is it not an act of self-castration, merely bolstering bourgeois institutions?

Raymond Williams offers the most balanced view: 'We have to establish the fringe culture—there is no alternative to that—but if we don't also contest the central institutions, we are giving away too much.' A too easy metaphor would be that there is a pincer movement at work amongst the working-class and amongst the bourgeois audiences. That would disguise the questions of quality and technique that confront the individual writers and groups. In other words, given the nature of the different audiences, what exactly is the effect desired, for it is scarcely a worthwhile exercise demonstrating the virtues of class solidarity to the average West End theatregoer.

Such is the principal question to ask of Bond, Griffiths, Barker, Brenton and Hare. In the statements in Ms Itzin's book we find too few direct answers. Individual approaches are justified but the ultimate object in terms of the chosen audience is not made clear often enough. Recourse to notions of 'art' walks too easily into the snares of the Council that bears that name, with its 'high' and 'low' aesthetics. Roy Shaw is quoted in a chapter on subsidy: 'By all means let us develop arts at a less demanding popular level; but to dismiss as elitist the subsidizing of the great works of the past or the often 'difficult' works of contemporary artists is to condemn the lock on the door to enrichment because you have failed to give people a key that fits it.' Such a view takes no account of the political consciousness and action necessary to obtain such a 'key', and simplistically relegates creativity to the level of object or icon. (Contrary to Koestler's concept, the ultimate task of Socialism is not access to 'art', but to creativity.)

For the agitprop or community groups, the question of intent is more readily answered, but the question of quality is perhaps more difficult, given the less comfortable environment in which the work is done. There is a sense of failure in David Edgar's turning from agit-prop to social realism and the established network. Itzin writes of its failure 'to reach and convert or mobilize the mass of the population.' With financial circumstances liable to worsen, and economic 'drawing-power' likely to be an essential criterion, the words of Roland Muldoon have a prophetic ring: 'Unions have had the virtuous socialist theatre groups, now they're pissed off and they want entertainment.' That does not preclude, and indeed should demand intelligent ideas.

In a sense, the story of political theatre in the seventies reads like a cultural footnote to Perry Anderson's *Considerations on Western Marxism*.

In two ways it directly substantiates his conclusions. Firstly, the extent to which Marxists since the time of Lukacs have been drawn/driven into cultural, literary activity—which, in the directly active context of theatre work is by no means as pessimistic a development as Anderson implies in discussing the academic work of contintal theorists. Secondly, what is more disturbing, the extent to which such activity has taken place in a climate of defeat. Mercer, Wesker, Barker and Griffiths all refer to the lack of a revolutionary situation in Britain and the lack of any popularly-based party addressing itself to such a cause. In these circumstances the theatre-worker is bound to be confronted with dilemmas. In setting out the individual histories and arguments of writers and companies (in necessarily limited space) Ms Itzin has contributed to their resolution; for whatever the difficulties of economy or authority, an essential unity remains clear in the desire to achieve, in the words of John McGrath: 'the realization of the full potential of every individual human life.'

MB

ENGLISH DRAMA: A Critical Introduction by Gámini Salgádo
(Edward Arnold; £11.50 cb, £4.95 pb)

One day there will be a critical guide that really will deserve all the usual recommendations that are freely heaped upon it. This is not an exception; it is a minimalist study which is brief without being either concise or comprehensive, and cannot hope to serve the needs of academics or even secondary school pupils. A thumbnail sketch of the major literary figures from the middle-ages to 1970 is weak meat, but if your appetite is lean, the work is easy to read and scattered with historical detail and anecdote. Nonetheless, since Salgádo makes no exaggerated claims for his work, it is to be valued as a kind of extended—though, sadly, not illustrated—encyclopaedia article.

DR

NEW PLAYS FROM JOHN CALDER

Nathalie Sarraute *Collected Plays* £4.95 ppr

These five plays translate Nathalie Sarraute's experimental techniques onto the stage. They are plays that dramatize inter-personal
and inter-social relationships, refining subtlety and nuance to an
incredible degree, and depicting the ways in which human beings
influence each other, and the antagonisms and irritations that we all
experience, often without knowing why. The confrontations of
generations, of different class, aesthetic or educational backgrounds,
the ways in which we come to understand each other, despise each
other, deceive each other, is the raw material of these plays, all of
which have been successfully staged in France by the
Renaud-Barrault Company

Translated by Maria Jolas and Barbara Wright, the volume contains
It Is There, It's Beautiful, Izzum, The Lie, Silence.

Howard Barker £4.95 ppr
That Good Between Us/Credentials of a Sympathizer

That Good Between Us is set in Britain under a Labour government,
perhaps slightly in the future. The unconstitutional and arbitrary use
of power by the Home Secretary, the conduct of the police and their
informers and treatment of 'subversive' elements are in line with the
direction in which our society is moving.

Credentials of a Sympathizer has a similar theme, the relationship
between the army and the 'terrorists' who oppose them at a time
when the latter are in a position to negotiate terms. Written before
the events leading to the birth of Zimbabwe, and at a time when the
powers of the guardians of authority are escalating, the play is
topical and urgent in its relevance.

Howard Barker £4.95 ppr
The Love of a Good Man/All Bleeding

The Love of a Good Man is about war and the class conflict which
underlies the great military confrontations and massacres of our time.
From the bleak landscape of a war cemetery at Passchendaele in 1920,
the author constructs a picture of the attitudes that survived and the
different and conflicting motivations of officers, men and the families
whose lives and outlook have been torn to pieces by events.

All Bleeding throws into contrast two phenomena of contemporary
society, the urge to die and escape from an unsavoury world, and the
life force that often finds its outlet in the desire to kill or be killed.
Three attempted suicides in the course of a few minutes overwork the
Metropolitan River Police, while members of a teenage judo club—the
violence of their instruction fresh in their ears—watch and cheer.

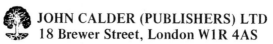 **JOHN CALDER (PUBLISHERS) LTD**
18 Brewer Street, London W1R 4AS

THEATRE DIARY

First the bad news . . .

Over dinner the other night (if I had said 'in my honour' that would
have demanded incriminating revelations) it suddenly came over
me. . . in the whole gathered company, I was the only person never to
have been to the United Status (sic). Now, you may think this would
be enough to make me stuff my holdall and heave off to Gatwick.
Not a bit of it. After ruminating unnoticed for a while I remembered
that it was I, after all, who best knew how to turn my own idiosync-
racies to some advantage. I interjected among some standard banal
talk about black women gay Irish writers: 'Well, of course, one must
accept that it's really rather chic these days to have a monochrome
TV, to never have been across the Atlantic and to despise video,
Prestel and Space Invaders.' A look of horror shot across my host's
face. 'I think it's obviously something that can quite set you apart
from the crowd. I mean, you can see the worst of America on your
own doorstep these days.' I wasn't referring of course to the rash of
MacDonalds so much as to the gush of sub-standard musicals
guaranteed to provide a 100% tax write-off in 2 acts and a twenty-
minute interval. They were aghast. 'Just look at Broadway: *Frankenstein*
opened for one night, then closed. And what do you make of our own
Biograph Girl, Barnardo, The Umbrellas of Cherbourg, The Beatles
and the rest. What we need is a formula that works—never mind
The Greatest Little Whorehouse in Texas and *42nd Street*, I'm
putting my money on a fantastic new family show written by that
great guy T.B. Oliet. It's called *Rats* and it has a cast of about fifty
with songs you can really sing along to. . . at last.'
  This kind of talk didn't seem to be having much impression, so I
ventured, those who had faith ought to show it by launching Andy
Rice-Paper's new marathon hit with a little of their own greenbacks.
Stunned silence. What the hell did I mean anyway that any goddam
show about rodents was supposed to be family entertainment.
Hadn't they heard? Kids love this kind of thing, I cried—what
about *Dr Who and the Elephant Man.* They groaned. 'Aw, come on
chaps, we're talking about a home-grown product, singing and
dancing, clean guys and gals falling in love: there'll be nothing like it
in years.' 'Sure there will,' said the fatter than average homely

person sitting a little too close to me. 'Whaddayamean,' I bark. 'You jus'
ain't heard, did ya sonny?' 'Heard what?'

Well, I was a fool to offer him the password to giving me a lesson in how
to trample somebody under the weight of a suit full of havana cigars. This
guy laid it on thick and came on pretty damn strong. Hadn't I heard of that
damn great guy Ross Taylor. Why dat guy made 7½ million big ones from
The King and I. An' whaddaya think he's doin' next? I should have guessed.
Yea, dat's it—*De Soun o' Muzak* wid Petoola. Could he truly be talking of
our own sweet Miss Clark? He could . . .and he was. This was going to be a
'spenderama', a 'superola', a 'sounderific'. And I guess he was right when I
heard later that the Apollo had installed a computerized avalanche, that
the Victoria buffet was selling Swiss munch packs and that Trapp
Traveller Train Tariffs were now being offered to anyone who didn't mind
sharing a compartment with Jimmy Savile.

And with those thoughts swirling round my confused head, I ran to
catch the next stopper to Worthampton to be in time for a performance of
Salad Days by the Civic Hall Players. Sweet charity.

. . . then the good news

It has been a good year for the London theatre-goer, not that it was easy
getting to see the really hot shows, so quickly did they sell out. However,
I finally managed to catch up with Peter O'Toole's wildly ambitious
Macbeth at the Carshalton Odeon 3: 'Is that a dagger I see before me, or
are you just glad to see me?' Did it give him clues for the wart-ridden tyrant,
Tiberius, in the film *Caligula*? Then I finally managed to squeeze into *Bums
in Britain*, only to find that it really was about homosexual rape, like they'd
said all along. The third time I went, they still hadn't removed the dirty
scenes, and my pals from the ballroom dancing club were so appalled
(especially the ones who brought their mothers) that we very nearly
considered walking out once the buggery bit was over.

But apart from that it must be said, a sumptuous production. And
indeed, it was during the interval of this very play, congregating in the lav
for some relief, I thought I saw an advert for an up-coming production
called *Mind the Step* by an old stalwart of the stage, too little seen or heard
of these days, T.S. Eliot. Imagine my surprise on realizing his name is an
anagram of Toilets. Such incidents only serve to underline the insidious
effects that repeated watching of homosexual rape can have on one.

Seriously, though, it might be best to view 1980 as a company year:
the best things seemed to come in packages. Obviously *Nicholas Nickleby*
was a company epic played with immense company passion, skill and
exuberance. The RSC *Three Sisters* arrived in London with a flawless
team from which it is almost unfair to single out Suzanne Bertish as
Masha. The Cottesloe Company under Bill Bryden's meticulous direction
provided deliberately slow, moving productions of O'Neill and Miller,
and continued the successful promenade performances. Peter Gill's gay,
gymnastic *Julius Caesar* (Riverside) and Richard Cottrell's magical

A Midsummer Night's Dream (Bristol Old Vic) were the result of good company playing under inspired directors. Of the visiting companies the Australian Nimrod Theatre presented the tight, fast, punchy Williamson play *The Club* at the Hampstead Theatre, and a Russian *Richard III* by the Rustaveli Company settled at the Roundhouse. Arise and conquer, oh 1981.

From our own correspondent

Sir Roy Shaw   22 December 1980
The Arts Council
105 Piccadilly
London W1

Sir,
I write to you in utter dismay about the Arts Council's recent handling of cuts in funding, with particular reference to Gambit.

We are surely not alone in deploring the procedure with which these cuts have been carried out: we had not been informed that our grant was threatened, we have had no time to seek alternative methods of funding in order to pay forthcoming invoices, and we are in a most difficult position vis-à-vis authors who have been commissioned for work well into 1981.

It has always been assumed that the work of the Arts Council was to provide financial assistance to those areas where there was no interest and no hope of becoming a commercial medium—whether this is dependent on sales or advertising. Such is the case with Gambit, which, having been established for fifteen years, is the oldest theatre journal in the country. To suggest that you have cut our grant on the grounds of diminished 'artistic or creative merit' really sounds like a poor joke, or an open confession of absolute shortsightedness on the part of your assessors. Since its inception Gambit has achieved wide critical support, has published the work of many young playwrights who have developed into major figures of our literary generation, and has been internationally distributed. That we fail to make a profit, and that we do not manage to pay our staff and contributors adequately need not be condemned; that is a state of affairs which we would right if we could . . . but instead we prefer to devote our energies to quality, topicality and to providing a medium in which new writing [both critical and dramatic] can emerge in a forum provided *nowhere* else in this country at this time.

That you have at the same time cut your funding to Theatre Quarterly and Theatre Notebook smacks of the truly ridiculous—the action of your institution will be deservedly mocked by academics, theatre professionals and anybody concerned with the growth of ideas in drama. Our right to exist has been denied because we cannot provide both the money we require and maintain the standards we have worked so hard to achieve. But perhaps to make an appeal on the grounds of 'justice' would be naive; what you must, however, acknowledge is that you have now brought to an end one highly respected area of critical writing: the literary journal dealing exclusively with theatre and the performing arts. May that be inscribed on the Arts Council's roll of honour.

Burbage

AMONG OUR CONTRIBUTORS

Tim Brassell produced *Artist Descending a Staircase* for the Sherman Arena Theatre in Cardiff before taking up a post as Publicity Officer for Northern Arts.

Anne-Marie Glasheen is currently preparing the translation of five Belgian plays for publication by John Calder (Publishers) Ltd.

David Gollob, after the stresses of contributing drama reviews to Gambit and elsewhere, has retired to Italy, whence it is hoped will emanate his next opus magnum.

Dougald McMillan, formerly of the University of North Carolina, has just completed (with Martha D. Fehsenfeld) a study of Beckett directing Beckett.

Judy Simons is a lecturer in English literature at Sheffield City Polytechnic.

Kenneth Tynan, who died in 1980, will best be remembered as one of Britain's finest and most influential drama critics, although he produced several plays, including his own *Oh! Calcutta*.

We acknowledge with gratitude the loan of photographs from Faber and Faber, The National Theatre, Genista Streeten, The Royal Shakespeare Company, The Young Vic.

DAVID MERCER: COLLECTED TV PLAYS

The tragic death of David Mercer in 1980 brought to an end the remarkable career of a writer whose influence on post-war dramatic art has not yet been fully realized. He was the first to see that there is a fundamental difference between plays for the stage and for TV and to bring a documentary approach to his work, mirroring his own times, their preoccupations, events and fears.

Volume One

Where the Difference Begins
A Climate of Fear   *The Birth of a Private Man*

The three long plays in this volume come directly out of his personal experience, reflecting his working class Yorkshire background and the family tensions between the new generation, educated and anxious to get out into the world, and the old with its loyalties to class and marxism. They document the civil disobedience of the anti-nuclear movements of the fifties, the escalation of the cold war, symbolized for many by the building of the Berlin Wall. As such they are an imaginative and true record of a significant period of recent history. Their effect was electric when first seen, and today are classics that have changed the course and the possibilities of TV drama. That they can be highly enjoyable to read has been discovered by many, and this new edition of the three plays that make up *The Generations* is intended for the permanent bookshelf. (£6.95 cased & £3.95 paper)

Volume Two

The Parachute   *A Suitable Case for Treatment*
Let's Murder Vivaldi   *For Tea on Sunday*
In Two Minds   *And Did Those Feet*

The six plays in this volume are now established TV drama classics: *A Suitable Case for Treatment,* given here in its original version, was first seen in 1962 and later adapted with many changes for the cinema under the title *Morgan.* It is largely a self-portrait of the author who portrays himself as a gorilla-like wild man often out of control of his own impulses and emotions, and the plays that follow all combine naturalistic representations of contemporary living with techniques borrowed from surrealism and absurdist drama with which Mercer has often been linked. His interest in psychiatry and the theories of R.D. Laing are particularly evident with *In Two Minds,* because Mercer was fascinated by schizophrenia. Mercer's television plays are very different from the techniques of stage drama and read well on the printed page.

(£6.95 cased, & £3.95 paper)

JOHN CALDER (PUBLISHERS) LTD
18 Brewer Street, London W1R 4AS

STOCK PLAYS FROM JOHN CALDER

The following plays and playscripts, some of which were formerly published by Calder and Boyars, are now distributed exclusively by John Calder (Publishers) Ltd.

Plays

	Cloth	Paper

Arthur Adamov
Paolo Paoli — £4.95 & £1.95

John Antrobus
You'll Come to Love Your Sperm Test (New Writers 4) — £4.95 & £2.25

Fernando Arrabal
Plays Vol. 1 (Orison, Fando and Lis, The Car Cemetery, The Two Executioners) — £4.50 & £2.25
Plays Vol. 2. (Guernica, The Labyrinth, The Tricycle, Picnic on the Battlefield, The Condemned Man's Bicycle) — £4.50 & £2.25
Plays Vol. 3. (The Architect and the Emperor of Assyria, The Grand Ceremonial, The Solemn Communion) — £4.50 & T.O.P.

Samuel Beckett
Come and Go — 75p

Stewart Conn
The Burning — £2.25

Copi
Plays Vol. 1 — £4.75 & £1.95

Marguerite Duras
Three Plays (Days in the Trees, The Square, The Viaducts of Seine-et-Oise) — £4.95 & £1.95
The Rivers and the Forests (*contained in* The Afternoon of M. Andesmas) — £3.95
Suzanna Andler (*also* La Musica *and* L'Amante Anglaise) — £5.95 & £2.95

Eugene Ionesco
Three Plays (The Killer, The Chairs, Maid to Marry) — £1.25
Plays Vol. 1. (The Chairs, The Bald Prima Donna, The Lesson, Jacques) — £4.95 & £2.25
Plays Vol. 2. (Amédée, The New Tenant, Victims of Duty) — £4.95 & £2.50
Plays Vol. 3. (The Killer, Improvisation, Maid to Marry) — £4.95 & £2.25
Plays Vol. 4. (Rhinoceros, The Leader, The Future is in Eggs) — £4.95 & £2.50
Plays Vol. 5. (Exit the King, The Motor Show, Foursome) — £4.95 & T.O.P.
Plays Vol. 6. (A Stroll in the Air, Frenzy for Two) — £4.95 & £2.25
Plays Vol. 7. (Hunger and Thirst, The Picture, Anger, Salutation) — T.O.P. & £2.25
Plays Vol. 8. (Here Comes a Chopper, The Oversight, The Foot of the Wall) — £4.95 & £1.95
Plays Vol. 9. (Macbett, The Mire, Learning to Walk) — £4.95 & T.O.P.
Plays Vol. 10. (Oh, What a Bloody Circus, The Hardboiled Egg, *and* Ionesco and His Early English Critics) — £4.95 & £1.95

Robert McLellan
Jamie the Saxt — £4.95 & £1.95

David Mercer
Belcher's Luck — £3.95

René de Obaldia
Plays Vol. 1. (Jenusia *and* 7 Impromptus for Leisure)   £4.95 & £2.25
Plays Vol. 2. (The Satyr of La Villette, The Unknown General
    and Wide Open Spaces)   £4.95

Robert Pinget
Plays Vol. 1. (Dead Letter, The Old Tune *and* Clope)   £2.25
Plays Vol. 2. (Architruc, About Mortin *and* The Hypothesis   £4.95 & £2.25

German Expressionism

Georg Kaiser
Five Plays (From Morning to Midnight,
    The Burghers of Calais, The Coral, Gas I,
    Gas II)   £4.95 & £1.95

Carl Sternehim
Scenes From the Heroic Life of the Middle
    Classes (The Bloomers, Paul Schippel, The Snob,
    1913, The Fossil)   £4.95 & £1.95

Seven Expressionist Plays
Kokoschka, Oscar: Murderer Hope of Womankind/
    Kafka, Franz: The Guardian of the Tomb/
    Barlach, Ernst: Squire Blue Boll/Kaiser, Georg:
    The Protagonist/Stramm, August: Awakening/Brust,
    Alfred: The Wolves/Goll, Ivan: Methusalem   £4.95 & £1.95

Vision and Aftermath
Goering, Reinhard: *Naval Encounter*
Hasenclever, Walter: *Antigone*
Hauptmann, Carl: *A Te Deum*
Toller, Ernst: *Hinkemann*   £4.95 & £1.95

Frank Wedekind
The Lulu Plays and other Sex Tragedies (Earth Spirit,
    Pandora's Box, Death and Devil, Castle Wetterstein)   £4.95 & £2.75

Playscripts

John Antrobus
Trixie and Baba   £3.50 & £1.95
Why Bournemouth? (*also* An Apple a Day, The Missing Links)   £3.50 & £1.95

Jane Arden
Vagina Rex *and* The Gas Oven   £3.50 & £1.95

Antonin Artaud
The Cenci   £2.95

Howard Barker
Fair Slaughter   £1.50
Stripwell *and* Claw   £6.50 & £3.25
That Good Between Us (in Gambit 31)   £2.00

Stan Barstow
An Enemy of the People   £1.50

Wolfgang Bauer
All Change, Party for Six, Magic Afternoon £4.95 & £2.25

Steven Berkoff
East (*also* Agamemnon, The Fall of the House of Usher) £4.95 & £2.25

Edward Bond
Early Morning £4.50 & £1.95

Howard Brenton and others
Lay By £3.50 & £1.95

Alan Brown
Skoolplay £1.50
Wheelchair Willie (*also* Brown Ale With Gertie, O'Connor) £5.95 & £2.95

Stewart Conn
The Aquarium (*also* The Man in the Green Muffler *and* £4.95 & £2.25
   I Didn't Always Live Here)

A.F. Cotterell
The Nutters (*also* Social Service or All Creatures Great and £3.50 & £1.95
   Small, *and* A Cure for All Souls)

Ian Curteis
Long Voyage Out of War (The Gentle Invasion, Battle at £3.95 & £1.95
   Trematangi, The Last Enemy)

Roland Dubillard
The House of Bones £3.50 & £1.95
The Swallows £2.95 & £1.95

Stanley Eveling
The Balachites, (The Strange Case of Martin Richter) £3.50 & £1.95
Come and Be Killed, *and* Dear Janet Rosenburg, £3.50 & £1.95
   Dear Mr. Koonig
The Lunatic, The Secret Sportsman, The Woman Next Door, £3.50 & £1.95
   and Vibrations

Paul Foster
Balls (*also* Hurrah for The Bridge, The Recluse *and* £4.50 & £1.95
   The Hessian Corporal)
Elizabeth 1 (*also* Satyricon *and* The Madonna in the Orchard) £3.95 & £1.95
Heimskringla! or The Stoned Angels £3.50 & £1.95
Marcus Brutus (*also* The Silver Queen) £5.50 & £2.25
Tom Paine £3.50

Tom Gallacher
Mr. Joyce Is Leaving Paris £1.95

Peter Gill
The Sleepers Den *and* Over Gardens Out £3.50 & £1.95

Trevor Griffiths
Occupations *and* The Big House £3.95

Roger Howard
Slaughter Night £3.50 & £1.95

Sandro Key-Aberg
O *and* An Empty Room £3.50 & £1.95

Tom Mallin
Curtains   £3.50 & £1.95

Eduardo Manet
The Nuns   £3.50 & £1.95

Robert McLellan
The Hypocrite   £3.50 & £1.95

David Mowat
Anna-Luse (*also* Jens *and* Purity)   £3.50 & £1.95
The Others   £3.50 & £1.95

Obaldia, René de
Wind in the Branches of the Sassafras   £3.50 & £1.95

Pablo Picasso
Desire Caught By the Tail   £3.50 & £1.95
The Four Little Girls   £3.50 & £1.95

Jan Quackenbush
Calcium (*also* Victims *and* Once Below a Time: three plays   £3.50 & £1.95
   for child actors including Coins, The Good Shine, Broken)
Inside Out (*also* Talking of Michelangelo *and* Once Below a   £3.50 & £1.95
   Time: three plays for child actors including Still Fires,
   Rolly's Grave, Come Tomorrow)

Nathalie Sarraute
Silence *and* The Lie   £3.50 & £1.95

David Selbourne
Samson *and* Alison Mary Fagan   £3.50 & £1.95

Roland Topor
Leonardo Was Right   £1.50

Frank Wedekind
Spring Awakening   £3.95 & £1.95

Vivienne C. Welburn
Clearway   £3.50 & £1.95
Johnny So Long *and* The Drag   £3.50 & £1.95
The Treadwheel *and* Coil without Dreams   £4.95 & £2.25

Heathcote Williams
The Immortalist   £1.50
AC/DC   £4.95

Colin Wilson
Strindberg   £3.50

Snoo Wilson
Pignight *and* Blow Job   £3.95   £1.95

Olwen Wymark
The Gymnasium (*also* The Technicians, Stay where You are,   £3.50 & £1.95
   Jack the Giant-Killer *and* Neither Here Nor There)
Three Plays (Lunchtime Concert, Coda, The Inhabitants)   £3.50